Mine Run:
A Campaign Of Lost Opportunities

October 21, 1863 -May 1, 1864

2nd Edition

Martin F. Graham   George F. Skoch

Manufactured in the United States by
H. E. Howard, Inc., Lynchburg, Virginia

Printed by H. E. Howard, Inc.

ISBN-0-930919-48-3

This book is lovingly dedicated
to our families
who have weathered the hardships of
our campaign like the
heartiest of veterans

ACKNOWLEDGEMENTS

Foremost on the list of all those who have played a significant role in creating this work is Harold E. Howard. His support, guidance, encouragement, and patience were welcome guideposts which we thankfully utilized throughout the process of completing this book.

Robert K. Krick, chief historian of the Fredericksburg National Military Park, is an invaluable resource for anyone studying the Confederate Army of Northern Virginia. As always, he was generous in his suggestions and assistance in this endeavor.

William D. Henderson, professor of history at Richard Bland College, helped to get us started on the right foot by directing us to the major repositories of Confederate manuscripts.

For anyone involved in historical research, the local library is often an untapped treasure. In our case, the staff of the Cleveland Public Library were extremely helpful, particularly Philip Ferguson and the members of his Inter-Library Loan Department; and Joanne Petrello, Christopher Wood, and all their associates in the History Department. Without their cooperation, this book would not have been possible.

Warren Ernst, his family, Mr. and Mrs. Harold M. Pearson, and the many other individuals who were extremely kind and helpful during our research trips to Virginia.

There were many others who were helpful in various ways. We wish to express our thanks to all who assisted us in this rewarding endeavor.

August 21, 1987   Martin F. Graham
                                                       George F. Skoch

Best wishes
Warren Ernst

CHAPTER I

"A Most Brilliant Feat of Arms"

In the early morning chill of the 15th of October, 1863, a somber Confederate Lieutenant General Ambrose Powell Hill led General Robert E. Lee onto an open field littered with scores of unburied corpses clothed in ragged butternut and gray uniforms. These were Hill's soldiers strewn about the rough terrain along the railroad embankment near Bristoe Station, Virginia; fine veteran fighters of Brigadier Generals John R. Cooke's and William W. Kirkland's North Carolina Brigades, killed the day before in a lopsided fire fight with three divisions of Federal riflemen sheltered behind the railroad grade. The slaughter was fearful — Hill's loss totaled about 1,400 men and five guns, Union casualties fewer than 600.[1]

Silently, Lee listened to Hill's account of the battle as the two officers guided their horses through the grisly autumn harvest. Hill was apologetic. He blamed himself for the failure, admitting he had ordered the attack without making a thorough reconnaissance beforehand. Major General Henry Heth's Division had walked into a virtual trap.

Hill had no sound explanation for his costly error in judgement except that he thought his troops had cornered the weak rearguard of Union Major General George Gordon Meade's retreating Army of the Potomac. Heth's division was totally unprepared, therefore, when the entire Federal II Corps suddenly appeared, undetected, and slammed fire into its right flank. Now Hill answered for his fatal lapse in generalship to his commanding officer, surrounded by the twisted and broken human wreckage of the bitter encounter. When Hill finished, Lee finally spoke.

"Bury your poor dead," he said grimly, "and say nothing more about it."[2] This was as strong a rebuke as a subordinate would ever hear from Lee.

The 56-year-old Confederate commander found it increasingly difficult to overlook costly mistakes by his subordinates. During the first year of his command, he had seemed to experience nothing but success. The situation drastically changed in July 1863, however, with the heartbreaking failure of the Pennsylvania Campaign, after which Lee unsuccessfully attempted to resign. In the past, he had been able to depend on Lieutenant General Thomas J. "Stonewall" Jackson to achieve a brilliant tactical strike when necessary, but Lee's "right arm" had now been dead five months. Even his "Old War Horse" and most trusted confidant, Lieutenant General James Longstreet, was not with him, his corps having been temporarily transferred to the Western Theater.

Until Longstreet returned, Lee had no choice but to depend on the abilities of his two newest corps commanders, Hill and Lieutenant General Richard S. Ewell. The 37-year-old Hill and 46-year-old Ewell, West Point graduates, had both shown much promise leading divisions, but neither had yet distinguished himself in higher command. The previous day's action at Bristoe Station was just the latest example of what could happen when too much responsibility was placed in inexperienced hands.

As Lee rode off the field with his brooding Third Corps commander, he could not hide the disappointment he felt in this latest setback.

Later that morning, Lee wrestled with his options. His scouts reported that Meade's army was entrenching farther north, outside Centreville, Virginia. Never one to give up the initiative of an offensive, Lee weighed the advantages of turning the Federal position and forcing Meade back to the defenses of Washington, ridding as much of Northern Virginia as possible of the enemy throughout the upcoming winter.

Painfully, however, Lee recognized the shortcomings of his weakened army. He never questioned his men's willingness to follow him wherever he led, but supplies were drawing perilously low. The quartermaster corps had failed to issue the army an adequate number of shoes, overcoats, and blankets, making the men ill-equipped for the rough Virginia roads and cold October nights.

Unprepared, therefore, for a sustained campaign, Lee reluctantly decided to shorten his supply line by falling back south of the Rappahannock River. To retard any attempt by Meade to follow as they retreated south, the Confederates destroyed more than twenty miles of the Orange and Alexandria Railroad, the lifeline of this section of Virginia.

Arriving at Rappahannock Station, a hamlet astride the railroad, around noon of October 18, Lee's army crossed the river and quickly settled into camp for what the men hoped would be an uneventful winter respite. Unknown to even the opposing commanders, however, much more action was in store for their armies before either side could finally settle into winter's routine.

Four Yankee officers galloped up the pike from Warrenton to the train station in Gainesville, Virginia, on Thursday morning, October 22. General Meade, his chief of staff, Major General Andrew A. Humphreys, and two aides hurried to catch the military train to Washington, for the Federal commander had an appointment with President Abraham Lincoln that afternoon.

Hurriedly entering the station, Meade headed straight for a small room used as a telegraph office. He quickly changed from his dusty uniform and boots, worn during several months of active campaigning, to a new coat, expensive trousers, and a pair of shoes, a more appropriate outfit for one of his infrequent meetings with his Commander-in-Chief.[3]

The 48-year-old West Point graduate had only been in command of the Army of the Potomac for less than four months but had already accomplished a feat which had escaped the grasp of several of his predecessors — defeating Robert E. Lee. In fact, Meade's spectacular victory at Gettysburg, Pennsylvania, was fought within the first week of his assuming command. Since those three days in July, however, his fortunes had been on the decline.

The plaudits this new hero of the war received for his success at Gettysburg were tempered by Congressional expressions of discontent over the fact that the Confederate army was permitted to escape, practically unopposed, south of the Potomac River. Heading the list of those disappointed with Meade's failure to crush Lee's force was the President.

Following the return of both armies to Virginia, Lincoln, through his general-in-chief, Major General Henry W. Halleck, who the President regarded as "little more than a first rate clerk,"[4] prodded Meade to strike a powerful blow against the enemy, who had taken up a defensive position south of the Rapidan River.

Unsure of the size of the enemy force and having just transferred 20,000 men, two corps, to the Western Theater, Meade was satisfied to limit his army's activity to monitoring the enemy along the Rapidan. As Lee began his Bristoe Campaign, the Federal commander's primary objective was not to confront Lee's troops, but to fall back as quickly as possible to prevent the Confederates from coming between his army and Washington. Lincoln found this passive response to Lee's aggressive campaigning very disconcerting.

When Meade failed to follow up his initial success against Hill's corps at Bristoe Station, deciding instead to take a defensive posture, Lincoln resolved to take a much more direct approach to spur his conservative commander to action. Under the guise of a telegram from Halleck, his mouthpiece, Lincoln communicated his dissatisfaction with Meade's performance. "Lee is unquestionably bullying you," Halleck wired his subordinate on October 18.[5]

The sensitive Meade, easily offended by even less direct criticism, confided in his aide, Colonel Theodore Lyman: "I used to think how nice it would be to be Commander-in-Chief; now at this moment, I would sooner go, with a division, under the heaviest musketry fire, than hold my place!"[6]

Meade realized, however, that he had the upper hand over his superiors in Washington. After all, no other Union commander had achieved his degree of success against the seemingly invincible Confederate Army of Northern Virginia. ("What can I do, with such generals as we have?" Lincoln exclaimed to an inquiry about relieving Meade. "Who among them is any better...?"[7]) The recalcitrant Federal general refused to accept passively this criticism from Halleck. "I take this occasion to repeat what I have before stated," he immediately replied, "that if my course, based on my own judgment, does not meet with approval, I ought to be, and I desire to be, relieved from command."[8] Lincoln most likely wished that his general would show this much spirit when confronting Lee.

His hand played, Meade did not have long to wait for the general-in-chief's reply. "If I have repeated truisms," Halleck, attempting to make amends for his less than tactful comments, wired at noon the next day, "it has not been to give offense, but to give to you the wishes of the Government. If, in conveying these wishes, I have used words which were unpleasing, I sincerely regret it."[9]

The apology accepted, Meade continued to ponder his next move against his Confederate opponent. An essential step in any plan of pursuit was reconstructing the Orange and Alexandria Railroad, which Lee had destroyed from Bristoe Station to the Rappahannock River. Meade realized it would have to be the primary means of keeping his army supplied during its advance southward.

Time was on Meade's side, however, for although a spell of Indian Summer made further campaigning quite possible, the Federal commander feared the approach of winter. In only a matter of hours, the roads of Virginia could turn into bottomless quagmires. Less than a year earlier, a sudden onset of winter rain had sunk the hopes of one of his predecessors, Major General Ambrose Burnside, and had made him a laughing stock throughout the North as well as the South.

His reputation on the line, therefore, Meade suggested in a telegram to Halleck on the 21st that campaigning be suspended for the winter and that the army withdraw to the fortifications around Washington. Rattled by this latest example of Meade's conservative approach to command, Lincoln summoned him to Washington the next day for a strategy session.[10]

So Meade and his entourage relaxed in a private passenger car as best they could during the "rattling and bumping" ride to Washington. Arriving at the capital on the afternoon of October 22, Meade went straight to Halleck's office where the two generals held a "solemn pow-wow." They both then proceeded to the White House where they met with the President.[11]

"The President was, as he always is, very considerate and kind," Meade wrote to his wife the next day. "He found no fault with my operations, although it was very evident he was disappointed that I had not got a battle out of Lee."[12] This analysis of the meeting was an understatement, however, probably designed not to offend the sensibilities of Mrs. Meade. Actually, at one point during the meeting, Lincoln compared Meade's pursuit of Lee following the Battle of Gettysburg to "an old woman shooing geese across a creek."[13]

It being too late to return to camp that evening, although Meade wished to return to his troops as soon as possible, the general and his aides remained in the city that night and caught the earliest train out of the capital the next morning.

If the President, as Meade later maintained, agreed with him that "there was not much to be gained by any farther advance,"[14] it did not take long for the Commander-in-Chief to change his mind. On October 24, Halleck wired his subordinate: "The President desires that you will prepare to attack Lee's army."[15] Meade may have been stubborn at times, but it finally became extremely clear to him that he had no choice in this matter. Under the capable supervision of Colonel Daniel C. McCallum, Superintendent of Military Railroads, the Orange and Alexandria line was rebuilt by November 1 as far south as Warrenton Junction. The Federal army was moving in the direction of the Rappahannock River, but its commander had little idea of what to do once it got there.

While Lincoln coerced his reluctant general southward, Lee busily planned his defense of the area below the Rappahannock River. Although suffering from violent back pains,[16] an early symptom of the cardiac disease which would eventually cause his death in 1870, he spent long hours preparing for his antagonist's arrival. Even though Lee did not know Meade was being prodded to pursue his army, the Confederate commander's scouts kept him informed of the progress of the Federal reconstruction of the railroad.

While reluctantly willing to surrender the area north of the Rappahannock to Union control, Lee decided to oppose any attempt by the Yankees to cross the river. It is likely he chose the Rappahannock line for his defense in order to prohibit the Union army from spending the winter any farther south than necessary. The ravages of war in this section of Virginia had already proven costly to civilians, their possessions, and their land. One Richmond reporter described these counties as "a vast territory of ruin and desolation."[17]

The Confederate commander posted his army along the southern bank with Hill's Third Corps to the left of the Orange and Alexandria

Railroad and Ewell's Second Corps to the right.

The most vulnerable link in his chain of defense was a much-used crossing, Kelly's Ford, about five miles down river from Rappahannock Station.

The terrain southwest of the ford, about a square mile of cleared land which gently sloped to the river, was dominated by high wooded bluffs on the northern bank. Realizing that Meade would command the southern bank if he should plant artillery along this ridge, Lee decided that a prolonged defense of the ford would prove to be useless and costly.

The Confederate commander consequently elected not to contest an enemy crossing at this site. He established instead a more defensible line farther inland, beyond the range of Union guns north of the ford.

Another measure Lee took to counter the defensive weaknesses of Kelly's Ford and other less significant points along his line was to establish a bridgehead north of the river. Troops in this work would force Meade to divide his army, reducing the impact of an uncontested crossing at Kelly's Ford, and would give Lee the opportunity to neutralize either column.

The Confederate leader chose a site along the river near Rappahannock Station for his bridgehead. To link the outpost with his main line along the southern bank, Lee stretched a pontoon bridge across the river about 800 yards above the remains of the Orange and Alexandria Railroad trestle, which the Yankees had destroyed prior to their retreat earlier that month during the Bristoe Campaign. Since a dam had been constructed a short distance downriver, it was impossible to ford the Rappahannock in this area, placing a great burden on this single pontoon bridge.

The focal points of the bridgehead were two redoubts on adjacent hills west of the railroad. They had originally been designed earlier in the war by Lee's engineers to cover the northern approaches to the river, later redesigned by Union troops to face the south, and now slightly modified by Confederates once again to repulse an attack from the north. Atop the hill closest to the tracks, about 100 feet away, was an enclosed earthen fort. Approximately 400 feet to the left of this work was a larger redoubt enclosed on three sides, open on its southern face. A chain of rifle pits connected both forts and extended east and west from them along a ridge.[18]

The terrain behind the small redoubt dropped sharply to the river while a clear and gently sloping plain ran between the larger work and the river about 500 feet away. The entire Confederate line along the northern bank was about one mile long with its flanks anchored on the river.

Infantry and artillery works south of the Rappahannock supported the bridgehead, covered the approaches to the pontoon span, and bolstered the outpost's relatively unprotected right flank, one of the most vulnerable portions of the Confederate line. Under cover of the steep slopes of the railroad embankment, an attacking force could approach to within 100 feet of the smaller redoubt before being vulnerable to Confederate fire. Lee hoped that guns placed on the other side of the river could adequately protect this flank.

Although the redoubts and rifle pits provided protection for artillery pieces and garrisoned troops, their tactical value was questionable. When Lee's army reoccupied this position, engineers did not make extensive changes in the design. Artillery placed in the redoubts was limited in the area it could command due to inadequate mounting, leaving large portions of terrain on the northern plain uncovered.

The positioning of the rifle pits along the ridge west of the large redoubt was also faulty. They were dug on the southern slope, facing the river, far enough from the crest so that anyone standing up in the pit could barely look over to the other side. No ditches were placed on the northern slope, the direction from which the Federals were expected to attack. This engineering oversight gave the enemy troops the opportunity to approach to within a few yards of the Confederate line before becoming accessible targets.

Neither abatis nor any other obstructions were placed in front of the works to hinder an enemy assault. Defenders had to rely on fire power alone to repulse a Union advance.[19]

Both Lee and Ewell, whose corps was charged with defending this position, realized that the works along the northern bank were vulnerable in spots, but they also felt that the works were "adequate to accomplish the object for which they were intended."[20] Lee was confident that a brigade or two could repulse any force thrown against it since both flanks rested solidly on the river and attacking troops would be exposed to heavy concentrated artillery and infantry fire while they crossed the large open plain in front of the Confederate position.

The confidence felt by Lee and Ewell was not shared by all of their subordinates. Confederate Major General Jubal A. Early, whose division alternated with that of Major General Edward Johnson in the defense of the bridgehead, found much fault with the position. "The works on the north side of the river," he later observed in his official report, "were, in my judgement, very inadequate, and not judiciously laid out or constructed." They afforded "no obstacle in themselves to an attacking enemy, and only furnished a temporary protection to our troops."[21]

The strength of these works would soon be tested, for Lincoln was pushing the reluctant George Meade south to strike a blow against his Confederate adversary.

Contrary to the opinions of the President and General Halleck, Meade was not averse to attacking the Army of Northern Virginia. He desired, however, to dictate to Lee the terms of the engagement, both time and place, instead of permitting the crafty Confederate commander to have things all his own way. Meade realized that the latter was the major factor in the downfall of his predecessors.

During the first few days of November, the Federal commander desperately sought information which would give him an advantage over Lee. Although the Union army had achieved great success over the enemy at Gettysburg, Meade may not have felt up to the task of confronting Confederates on Southern soil. Only two weeks earlier, the Federal general admitted to his wife that Lee had outgeneralled him during the Bristoe Campaign. "This was a deep game," he wrote, "and I am free to admit that in the playing of it he has got the advantage of me."[22] It is no mystery, therefore, why Meade, who even in the best of times was very cautious, approached this offensive thrust very systematically.

Command of the Army of the Potomac had been taking its toll on the general. While in Washington on October 22, acquaintances observed that his "hair and beard were growing prematurely gray and that he was looking a little worn."[23]

Frustrated in his attempt to discover a weakness in the enemy line which he could effectively exploit, Meade suggested an alternate plan to the War Department. On November 2 he wired Halleck that his intelligence sources had informed him that Lee, with at least 4,000 reinforcements, had established a strong defensive position south of the Rappahannock from Sulphur Springs on the Confederate left to Kelly's Ford on the right. Assuming that an attempt to force a passage across the river would be extremely costly, Meade proposed a movement around the enemy right flank. He ruled out a swing around Lee's left because of the necessity of abandoning the railroad for dirt roads which in the early winter months could become mud pits within hours. Instead, Meade suggested that a thrust in the direction of Fredericksburg would have the greatest chance for success.

> ... I have determined to attempt the movement by [Lee's] right, throwing the whole army rapidly and secretly across the Rappahannock at Banks' Ford and Fredericksburg, and taking position on the heights [Marye's] beyond the town.

> ... My present position, and repairing the railroad, has doubtless induced [Lee] to believe I shall adhere to this line, and if my movement can be started before he is apprised of it, I have every reason to believe it will be successful, so far as effecting a lodgment on the heights in advance of him; and if he follows and gives me battle, my object will be accomplished.[24]

8

Meade also realized that his army could easily be supplied by either rail or water in this new position, which would assist in effecting a smooth transfer of base from Central Virginia. He had confidence in this plan and perceived it as a rare opportunity to gain a strategic advantage over his wily opponent.

Haunted by the memory of Burnside's disastrous defeat at Fredericksburg the previous December, and having little confidence in Meade's ability to deceive Lee, Lincoln rejected his general's proposed plan. "Any tactical movement to turn a flank or threaten a communication is left to your own judgement," Halleck wired Meade the next morning; "but an entire change of base under existing circumstances, I can neither advise nor approve."[25]

With all other options denied him, Meade once again studied Lee's line along the Rappahannock, looking very carefully for any weakness he could exploit to gain a foothold on the southern bank. By November 5, he developed a plan which he hoped would give him the advantage he sought.

The orders he circulated to his corps commanders the next day called for the creation of two wings. The right column would be led by the VI Corps commander, Major General John Sedgwick. The 50-year-old West Point graduate would direct his own and the V Corps. His wing was to advance at daybreak on November 7 from the vicinity of Warrenton to Rappahannock Station, a distance of about 16 miles.

The other wing of the Army of the Potomac was placed under the III Corps commander, Major General William H. French, 48 years old and also a graduate of West Point. In addition to French's corps, the I and II were to advance from the vicinity of Warrenton Junction to Kelly's Ford, about 17 miles away.

Cavalry divisions were assigned to cover each flank. The 1st Division, under Brigadier General John Buford, was placed on the army's right; Brigadier General H. Judson Kilpatrick's 3rd Division was to cover the left; and the 2nd Division of Brigadier General David McM. Gregg was to remain in reserve to guard the trains and lines of communication.[26]

Both wings were ordered to travel light, leaving unnecessary wagons and equipment behind, for the strength of Meade's plan lay in his army's ability to move quickly, giving the enemy little time to strengthen the points of attack.

Meade had confidence in his wing commanders. Sedgwick had a solid reputation as an intelligent and effective fighter since his assignment to the command of the VI Corps earlier that year. He was very popular with his men, who affectionately referred to him as "Uncle John."[27]

In contrast to Sedgwick's success in corps command, French had not yet been tested in this important role, having just been assigned the III Corps shortly after the Gettysburg Campaign. Although he had demonstrated considerable skill in division command at the battles of Antietam, in Maryland, and Fredericksburg, he had yet to prove himself in corps command. In less than a month, his great success at Kelly's Ford would be eclipsed by blunders which ultimately contributed to the failure of this campaign.

Believing that the task assigned to the left column had the greatest chance of success, Meade ordered French to push past the enemy at Kelly's Ford and, once across the river, assist Sedgwick in dislodging the Confederates from their Rappahannock Station bridgehead. Accomplishing this, the two columns were to move as quickly as possible to intercept the enemy at Brandy Station.

If he was unable to seize the Confederate works in his front, Meade directed Sedgwick to quickly withdraw to Kelly's Ford, cross there, and support French in his push toward Brandy Station.

French's III Corps began its march to Kelly's Ford at 5:00 a.m. on the 7th. By noon the leading elements of the column reached Mount Holly Church, about one mile northeast of the ford. Their arrival was masked from enemy observation by a high ridge, the southern edge of which overlooked the Rebel position south of the river.

The division assigned the task of defending the Confederate right flank belonged to Major General Robert E. Rodes, a 34-year-old graduate of the Virginia Military Institute. His troops occupied two lines of rifle pits with four-foot-high breastworks along the southern bank, in front of and to the right of the river crossing. On the morning of the 7th, the 2nd North Carolina Infantry, 322 men of Brigadier General Stephen D. Ramseur's Brigade, was deployed along the river, placed at Kelly's Ford and other nearby crossing points. The greater portion of the regiment remained in the immediate vicinity of the ford. The regimental commander, Lieutenant Colonel Walter S. Stallings, sent a small squad across to the northern bank, placed four companies in the rifle pits, and garrisoned the rest in and around the few buildings of Kellysville, a small community just west of the ford.

Another regiment of Ramseur's brigade, the 30th North Carolina Infantry, supported the Fluvanna Artillery of Captain John L. Massie which was deployed along the fringe of woods about three quarters of a mile west of the ford. The 500 men of this Tarheel regiment were commanded by Lieutenant Colonel William W. Sillers.[28] In the absence of General Ramseur, who was honeymooning in North Carolina, Colonel William R.

Cox of the 2nd led the brigade. (This 31-year-old former lawyer would have the dubious distinction of being wounded 11 times during the course of the war.)[29]

At noon on November 7, Cox notified his division commander that the enemy cavalry, which had been picketing the ford for several days, had been replaced by infantry. Rodes hurried to Kellysville to evaluate the situation personally. Not taking any chances, he ordered the remaining brigade commanders to place their troops in preassigned positions in woods west of the ford, the line running from the river to the Stevensburg Road. If the enemy was to attack, Rodes did not intend to be caught off guard.

His orders were to stall an enemy attempt to cross the river long enough to give the rest of his division time to occupy the line in the woods. He was to engage the fewest number of troops necessary to accomplish this task. Once the enemy crossed and Cox's men fell back to the division line, Rodes' troops were to stop a further Union advance until reinforcements arrived.

From an observation point east of the Rappahannock, French surveyed the enemy position and decided to assault the Confederates defending the ford with his infantry. As Lee had anticipated, the Union left wing artillery commander, Captain George E. Randolph, hurriedly placed his guns along the heights overlooking the ford to cover the Federal advance.

The 3-inch rifled ordnance of the 10th Massachusetts Battery, under Captain J. Henry Sleeper, was deployed on the ridge closest to the river and a half mile south of the ford. The 4½-inch Rodman guns of Captain Franklin A. Pratt's Battery M, 1st Connecticut Heavy Artillery, were placed along the heights on the south side of Marsh Run, a tributary of the Rappahannock. They commanded the ford as well as the open plain beyond Kellysville.

The 12-pound pieces of Battery E, 1st Rhode Island, under Lieutenant John K. Bucklyn, were deployed on a bluff north of Marsh Run. Six other batteries were assigned positions along the heights, behind and in support of these three batteries.

The brigade of Colonel P. Regis de Trobriand of the 1st Division, III Corps was assigned the task of leading the assault. The 47-year-old French-born officer was not a professionally trained soldier but had previously distinguished himself as an effective leader on a number of battlefields.

The 20th Indiana Infantry and the 2nd Battalion United States Sharpshooters were temporarily assigned to de Trobriand's command to assist in the assault.

As soon as they were in position, Sleeper's, Pratt's, and Bucklyn's batteries directed a concentrated fire on the Confederates in the rifle pits and effectively prevented the troops in Kellysville from reinforcing them. Sleeper and Pratt also silenced sharpshooters sheltered in a brick mill near the ford. The Federal fire was answered by Massie's Confederate battery, which had advanced from the woods, but it was only a short time until it too was silenced by concentrated fire from both Sleeper's and Bucklyn's guns.[30]

One witness to the effectiveness of the Federal fire stated: "Sleeper's battery, on authority of some prisoners, is said to have taken off the legs of some of the Rebel staff officers. Their horses were killed, and left upon the ground, to show the severity of the fire."[31]

Contrary to Lee's orders to engage only those troops necessary to temporarily stall a Federal crossing, Rodes ordered the 30th North Carolina forward in support of the beseiged 2nd. These seasoned veterans of Antietam, Gettysburg, and numerous other engagements were met by a storm of Union artillery fire. Forced back three times under the barrage, the men of the 30th finally broke in confusion and rushed to the nearest shelter, many taking refuge in the brick mill. While attempting to maintain some semblance of order in the ranks, Lieutenant Colonel Sillers was mortally wounded.[32]

Ignoring the orders of line officers to fall back to the safety of the woods, the Tarheels remained in their shelter. The prospect of retreating across the shell-torn open plain behind them in the face of deadly enemy fire was more disconcerting to them then what they might face by remaining in Kellysville.

Across the river, the 1st and 2nd U.S. Sharpshooters, commanded by Lieutenant Colonel Casper Trepp, advanced down the bluffs to the right of Pratt's battery, quickly forded Marsh Run, and rushed across the narrow plain between the heights and the riverbank in the face of intense enemy fire. The Confederate pickets north of the river fired one volley and then quickly withdrew to the rifle pits on the southern bank.

Concealing themselves behind trees, rocks, and a low ridge on the northern bank, the sharpshooters exchanged shots with the Tarheels for several minutes; the Federals, pin-point marksmen with scopes on their rifles, held a decided advantage. After several minutes, Trepp ordered the 1st Sharpshooters across the ford to storm the enemy works.

Many of the 1st Sharpshooters balked at the order, however, fearful of being caught helplessly in the middle of the cold, waist-deep river — easy targets for the Confederate riflemen. Their division commander, Major General David B. Birney, irritated by enemy fire directed at his staff grouped near Bucklyn's guns, finally resorted to language "not found in military tactics, or the church catechism" to coerce his reluctant soldiers into the water.[33]

Trepp chose to cross the rapids above the ford since this area was not directly in front of the Confederate rifle pits. Nevertheless, as his men plunged into the river, they met with stiff resistance from the Tarheel defenders hiding behind brush on the western bank. Many of the sharpshooters slipped as they rushed through the rapids, struggling to gain a footing and to push forward in the face of a hail of enemy lead. Others fell, their riddled bodies carried down the river by the strong current.

A sharpshooter later recounted the deadly crossing:

A volley, mowing down ten men, received us right upon setting foot in the river. However, we quickly pushed on and succeeded in getting below the line of fire of the Confederates who would now have to rise above the breastworks to aim at us, thereby exposing themselves to our comrades' bullets.[34]

Those sharpshooters who survived the crossing quickly captured the defenders who had failed to fall back. The Union force next turned its attention to the left flank of the entrenched Tarheels. As the Yankees rushed from one rifle pit to another they exchanged point blank shots with the enemy and, when close enough, engaged in fierce hand-to-hand fighting. Stubborn pockets of resistance were systematically overcome by the sharpshooters, who did not take long to capture the first line of rifle pits. A chronicler of the engagement described the frantic action:

The Michigan members [companies C and I] had run forward in advance, closely followed by other companies, and when within 10 feet of the first pit in their front, the enemy rising up, fired a volley, but, being above, fortunately shot too high and but few were struck. Our men at once charged on to them, capturing at this place about 80 — "packed in the bottom of the pit like sardines." . . . It was a lively scrimmage; but more so at the next pit, where through fire and smoke, mid groans and shrieks of wounded men, some bayoneted, others blown through by opposing rifles, the work was carried.[35]

Once the sharpshooters were in control of the first line of rifle pits, they were joined by the 2nd Sharpshooters and then the remainder of de Trobriand's brigade. They charged upon the second line of pits, then "without stopping," recalled the brigade commander in his memoirs, "we advanced on the village on the run. The enemy, who did not expect us there so soon, offered little resistance, and surrendered with a good grace."[36] Those Tarheels who had taken refuge in the brick mill were also

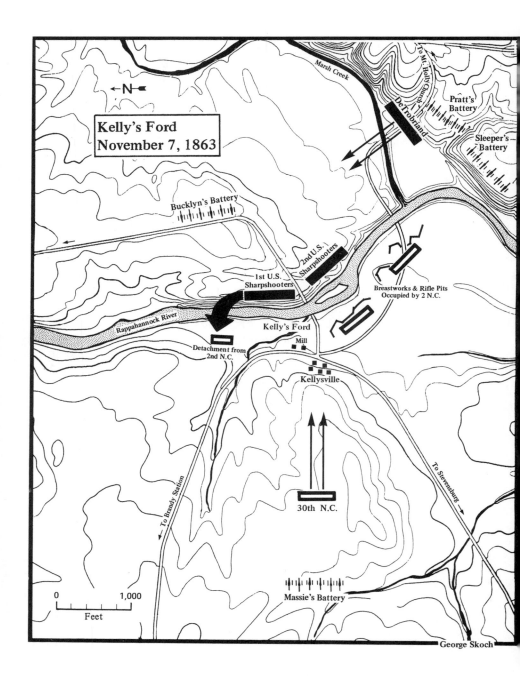

N

Kelly's Ford
November 7, 1863

Marsh Creek

To Mt. Holly Church

De Trobriand

Pratt's Battery

Sleeper's Battery

Bucklyn's Battery

2nd U.S. Sharpshooters

1st U.S. Sharpshooters

Breastworks & Rifle Pits
Occupied by 2 N.C.

Rappahannock River

Kelly's Ford

Mill

Detachment from
2nd N.C.

Kellysville

30th N.C.

To Brandy Station

To Stevensburg

0   1,000

Feet

Massie's Battery

George Skoch

14

quickly rounded up.

It was not long before the whole plain on the southern bank was in Union hands. By 3:00 p.m., Birney's entire division had crossed the ford and deployed within a few hundred yards of Rodes' position. Federal engineers hastily stretched two pontoon bridges across the river and by nightfall the entire III Corps had crossed. French deployed pickets as close to the enemy line as possible, but decided not to assault the Confederates until daybreak the next morning.

While French surveyed the situation in his front, Rodes strengthened his line and awaited a Union attack. Major General Edward Johnson's Division arrived after dark, moved to the right of Rodes' position, and extended the Confederate line from the river to Mountain Run.

During the day's fighting at the ford, French's troops inflicted heavy casualties on the two regiments of Ramseur's brigade. While losing only 42 men, the Federals killed, wounded or captured 330 men of the 2nd and 30th North Carolina, more than 40% of the Confederates engaged.[37]

Upon learning of the Union crossing at Kelly's Ford, Lee sent A. P. Hill orders to reinforce Rodes. He advised his feisty Third Corps commander to strike French the next morning and drive him back to the river, while Early's troops kept the Federal infantry at Rappahannock Station in check. Lee's plan was well conceived but based on what proved to be a false assumption — he had disastrously overestimated the strength of his works north of the river at Rappahannock Station, thereby jeopardizing the lives of more than two thousand irreplaceable Confederate soldiers.

As French was beginning his preparations for the assault on the enemy position at Kelly's Ford, Sedgwick's wing arrayed itself for battle on the outskirts of Rappahannock Station. The VI Corps deployed in woods to the right of the Orange and Alexandria Railroad and the V Corps to the left. Close to a mile of relatively flat, open ground separated the opposing lines.

While Sedgwick commanded the right wing of the Army of the Potomac, Brigadier General Horatio G. Wright, a 43-year-old West Pointer, was given temporary charge of the VI Corps. Wright's division, which was on the extreme left of the corps line with its left resting on the railroad, was assigned to Brigadier General David A. Russell. Also a West Point graduate, this 42-year-old officer had a reputation for exemplary leadership, often placing himself in the heart of the fiercest fighting. Command by example would prove successful for Russell on this day but would tragically result in his death, less than a year later, at the Third Battle of Winchester on September 19, 1864.[38]

15

Brigadier General Albion P. Howe, another military academy graduate and career officer, commanded the division to the right of Russell's. The 45-year-old general's force was strengthened by several regiments from Brigadier General Henry Terry's division, which was held in reserve.

Anchoring the left of the VI Corps line was Russell's brigade, under the command of Colonel Peter C. Ellmaker. To Ellmaker's right was the brigade of Brigadier General Joseph J. Bartlett, temporarily assigned to Colonel Emory Upton while the general commanded the 1st Division of the V Corps.

To the left of the railroad, the V Corps front was covered by 900 skirmishers under Brigadier General Kenner Garrard. The corp's three divisions formed in line of battle behind Garrard's command.[39]

The opposing forces were unusually quiet while front-line troops on both sides awaited orders. The historian of the 118th Pennsylvania of the V Corps remembered:

> The lines lay watching each other without exchanging shots. It was not intended ours should open, unless forced to, until the general advance began. The guns, too, remained silent, apparently awaiting opportunity for a better range.
>
> It was a stirring sight. The sun, slowly sinking, glistened on the bright barrels of the muskets far away to the left as the line swept around in a graceful curve almost to the river. Both regimental standards were unfurled, and there was wind enough to float them even when the line was not in motion. With all this taunt the enemy still maintained silence.[40]

The officers and men of the two Union corps studied the Confederate fortifications carefully. It was clearly evident that the enemy position was well-manned and formidable, making the success of a direct assault very questionable. As one of Sedgwick's staff officers, Major Charles A. Whittier, observed, "Rappahannock Station is a vile place to approach for attack. . . ."[41]

One indication that the Federals felt an attack would be costly was later recalled by a Confederate cannoneer observing their activities from across the river: "They must have anticipated immense slaughter, as no less than a hundred of their ambulances were plainly visible."[42] The anxiety of the Yankees contrasted sharply with the confidence of the Confederate infantrymen, who felt that they could defend themselves against any force the enemy threw against them.[43]

The self-assured Confederates who stood between Sedgwick and the river were the Louisiana Tigers of Brigadier General Harry T. Hays.

16

These battle-hardened veterans had relieved the equally renowned "Stonewall" Brigade in the works on the morning of November 6. Hays' troops were under the command of Colonel Davidson B. Penn while the general served on court martial duty. The 27-year-old colonel was a Virginia Military Institute graduate and former New Orleans businessman.

The Tigers had gained their well-deserved fame on numerous battlefields with the Army of Northern Virginia. Early could not have called on a more dependable unit to assume the responsibility of defending this important outpost. In fact, they most likely welcomed this opportunity to avenge their bloody repulse on Cemetery Hill during the evening of the second day's fighting at Gettysburg.

On the morning of November 7, the 6th Louisiana, commanded by Colonel William Monaghan, was on the right of the line, a quarter of a mile in advance of the works; the 9th Louisiana, under Colonel William R. Peck, was retained in the redoubts; to the left of the 9th were the 8th and 7th Louisiana, commanded by Captain A. L. Gusman and Lieutenant Colonel Thomas M. Terry respectively, both deployed along a ridge about a quarter of a mile from their fortifications. Possession of these heights was vital to the security of the forts since they were higher than the hills upon which the redoubts were constructed. Enemy artillery emplaced there would have an excellent field of fire into the Confederate works.

The remaining Tiger regiment, Captain J. G. Angell's 5th Louisiana, was on picket along the southern bank of the river about a half mile from the bridgehead.

Two guns of the Louisiana Guard Artillery, under Lieutenant Robert L. Moore, were in each of the redoubts. Two of the pieces were 10-pounder Parrotts while the other two were 3-inch ordnance guns.[44]

Cavalry pickets first informed Penn of the approach of Union infantry at about 11:00 a.m. on November 7. He ventured forward to the vedette post on the Warrenton Road and decided that the situation was serious enough to notify his divison commander, General Early, by dispatch at 11:45 a.m.

A second message was sent to Early at about 1:15 p.m. informing him that the enemy was in line of battle in woods along the Tigers' front, that Federal skirmishers had advanced a short distance from their main line, and that a larger enemy force — French's wing — had moved in the direction of Kelly's Ford.

At 2:00 p.m., Sedgwick advanced his forward line about 200 yards in front of the woods, followed a half hour later by the remaining lines of battle. For the Tigers, this movement was the first indication that they were being confronted by two enemy corps.[45]

17

To partially fill a large gap on his left flank, Penn called for the 5th Louisiana to cross the bridge and join the rest of the brigade. It fell into line between the 7th and 8th Louisana, which were still on the heights beyond the forts. Including the men of the Louisana Guard Artillery, there were now a few more than 900 Confederates north of the river facing almost 30,000 Federals.[46]

After studying the enemy position, Sedgwick realized that although it was strong, it possessed inherent weaknesses. Instead of storming the works, he determined it would be less costly but just as effective to drive the Confederates back into the fortifications with his infantry and then deploy his artillery on the heights before the enemy works. From this dominating position, a well-directed barrage from massed Union guns might be enough to drive the Confederates back across the Rappahannock.

The Federal line was ordered forward between 3:00 and 3:30 p.m. To the left of the railroad Garrard's skirmishers, supported by Bartlett's division, pushed the 6th Louisiana back into the main works. Garrard's force occupied about 800 yards of the northern bank and advanced to within a "short distance" of the enemy position along the railroad. "It was a glorious pageant of real war," the 118th Pennsylvania historian remembered. "Rarely is the sight seen of an advancing line so extended, all in view, and under fire at the same time."[47] The V Corps line curved around the Confederate works until its right, composed of troops from the 20th Maine Infantry, overlapped the VI Corps front for about 100 yards west of the railroad.

The Confederate artillery pits along the southern bank, which had been constructed to prevent an advance such as Garrard's troops had just accomplished, were not occupied. Before guns could be placed in these works, Union sharpshooters on the northern bank made deployment of artillery extremely dangerous, if not impossible.

While the V Corps drove the 6th Louisiana back into the works, the skirmish line of General Russell's division, on the other side of the railroad, crossed a mill stream, raced over an open plain under a destructive fire from Penn's troops and Moore's artillery, and took shelter behind a low ridge at the base of the hill which held the Confederate works. The Federals were now less than 250 yards away from the enemy redoubts.

Howe's division scaled the heights in its front, forcing the Tigers back into the rifle pits and larger redoubt. Three batteries were then deployed along the ridge overlooking and about 1,500 yards from the enemy fortifications. Together with two batteries behind the V Corps line, the Federal guns began to hammer the enemy forts and rifle pits.[48]

Generals Lee and Early arrived together at the works along the southern bank. They scaled a large hill to observe the situation across the river. While the Federals were driving the Tigers back into the fortifications, Early crossed the pontoon bridge to evaluate first hand the state of affairs. Discovering a large gap between the 8th and 5th Louisiana, the division commander rushed back across the river to hurry forward reinforcements to bolster Penn's line.

As the Union guns began lobbing shells into the Tigers' works, Lee directed the Rockbridge Artillery of Captain Archibald Graham and the Powhatan Artillery of Captain Willis J. Dance, both in redoubts across the river, to support Moore's guns. They quickly discovered, however, that the Union artillery was beyond the range of their batteries. The four overmatched guns of the Louisiana Guard Artillery alone responded to the Yankee fire as best they could.

Learning of the impending battle, General Hays rushed to the works occupied by his brigade. His arrival at about 4:00 p.m. coincided with the crossing of Brigadier General Robert F. Hoke's North Carolina Brigade. Following an exhausting double-quick march of seven miles from the vicinity of Culpeper, the Tarheels filed across the pontoon bridge and were led to the position which had been the gap in the Tigers' line. As they deployed in the rifle pits to the right of the 5th Louisiana, the North Carolinians were subjected to deadly artillery and infantry fire.

Since Hoke was still on leave, recovering from a wound received at Gettysburg, the Tarheels were commanded by Colonel Archibald C. Godwin. He placed Colonel Kenneth M. Murchison's 54th North Carolina on the left; the 6th, under Colonel Robert F. Webb, in the middle; and Lieutenant Colonel Hamilton C. Jones' 57th on the right, next to the 8th Louisiana.[49] The addition of Hoke's Brigade only slightly improved the Confederate odds north of the river. There were now about 2,000 men facing 30,000 Federals.[50]

Despite a lack of formal military training, General Hays, 43-years-old, had acquired valuable combat experience in the Mexican War. Since 1861, he had distinguished himself on battlefields from First Manassas to Gettysburg. The 32-year-old Godwin also lacked formal martial training; but, from his first taste of combat at the First Battle of Fredericksburg, he had earned for himself the reputation of a fighting officer with a knack for being where the bullets flew thickest. Like his adversary this day at Rappahannock Station, General Russell, this willingness to expose himself to enemy fire would lead to his death less than a year later at the Third Battle of Winchester.[51]

The Tarheels' arrival did not go unnoticed by General Sedgwick. Fearing that the enemy reinforcements might indicate that the Confederates were preparing to attack, he ordered General Russell to advance his division to within a short distance of its skirmish line.[52]

While both sides at Rappahannock Station were monitoring each other's movements and bracing for inevitable combat, Meade anxiously waited at his headquarters near Kelly's Ford for word from Sedgwick. Concerned that Lee might be massing troops to counterattack French's isolated bridgehead south of the Rappahannock, Meade feared that the III Corps would be engulfed by Lee's troops before Sedgwick could come to its assistance. With his two wings united, Meade could oppose Lee with a solid front. While helplessly waiting, the Federal commander could only hope that his subordinates were up to the tasks at hand.[53]

His right wing commander had been keeping a watchful eye on the effects of his artillery barrage. After almost three hours of shelling the Confederate works, however, and with darkness fast approaching, it became evident to Sedgwick that the Union guns alone would not be capable of dislodging the enemy. He decided that a direct infantry assault was his only resort.

Although the Confederate fortifications were still formidable, certain factors favored a Federal attack. The V Corps was solidly established on the enemy right and General Howe's division of the VI Corps was well-deployed on the Confederate left. With the Tigers' attention being focused on the flanks at the same time as they dodged Union shells, Sedgwick hoped the redoubts would be vulnerable to a direct twilight attack.[54]

Before ordering the attack, however, Sedgwick decided to seek the counsel of his VI Corps commander, General Wright. The exchange between the two officers was later recalled by Colonel Martin T. McMahon, the wing commander's chief of staff:

"Wright, what do you think are the chances for an assault with infantry on that position?"

"Just as you say, General," Wright noncommittally responded.

"What does Russell think about it?"

It so happened that the acting division commander approached the two at that moment.

"Here comes Russell," Wright answered; "he can speak for himself."

"Russell, do you think you can carry those works with your division?"

"I think I can sir," Russell answered quietly.

"Go ahead and do it," Sedgwick ordered.[55]

This exchange pointed out the uncertainty felt by these three general officers over their ability to take the Confederate works. No one, it seemed, wished to assume the final responsibility for ordering the assault.

The conversation recounted by Colonel McMahon strikingly contrasted with the other accounts of how the decision to attack was made. Russell's official report of the action gave a much different version of the events leading up to the Yankee assault:

> At sundown, after carefully considering the relative positions and the well-known character of my troops, it was my desire to storm the enemy's position, and a message was sent . . . to Brig. Gen. H. G. Wright, commanding the corps, asking permission to do so. That permission was granted. . . .[56]

To cloud the issue even more, in Wright's official report he suggested that it was his idea to attack the enemy works.[57]

No matter which account might be closest to the truth, once the decision was made to attack, little time was wasted in preparing for the assault. Russell assigned the responsibility for the attack to Ellmaker's brigade, which was already at the foot of the slope leading up to the enemy's works. Upton's brigade, on Ellmaker's right, was to advance in support. The combined strength of both of the brigades was about 2,120 men, roughly equal to the number of Confederates in the entire works.[58]

By coincidence or design, the 6th Maine, which occupied the brigade skirmish line, would bear the brunt of the attack. Not only was this regiment composed of muscular lumbermen; but, under similar circumstances, this courageous group of men was the first to storm successfully onto Marye's Heights at the Second Battle of Fredericksburg, six months earlier. As in that previous engagement they were ordered to fix bayonets, uncap their guns to prevent any misfirings, and charge the works without stopping to fire a shot. Officers emphasized that any hesitation during the attack could prove fatal in the face of enemy fire. The men of the 6th would be supported by the 5th Wisconsin, which also had been in the forefront during the earlier charge at Fredericksburg.[59]

Although the Tigers had not constructed abatis or any other impediments to deter the Federals during their attack, the area over which Ellmaker's troops were to charge was not without its obstacles. Russell evaluated the terrain in his official report:

> Upon the command "forward, double-quick," the skirmish line, with their support, dashed on in a style never surpassed by any troops. The ground was of a nature well calculated to check the impetuosity of a charge. Across the way as they advanced, the storming column encountered a formidable ditch, 12 or 14 feet wide, some 6 feet deep, and filled with mud and water to an average depth of 3 feet. Crossing this they came to a plain broken with stumps and underbrush, while before the skirmish line in the advance could be reached, a dry moat or ditch had to

be crossed, nearly as formidable as the obstacles already passed.[60]

As was his custom, Russell personally led the attack. The Union artillery kept up its fire until the last possible moment, opening a corridor through which the 6th Maine charged. Although it had been hoped that darkness and powder smoke would mask the assault, the men of the 6th were subjected to a destructive fire from the Confederate works. One Federal remembered:

> The fire grew heavier as the line neared the works, and the men were struck down with fearful rapidity, but unwavering, with wild cheers the survivors reached the fortifications, and springing over them, engaged the enemy in a hand to hand conflict. The enemy astonished and bewildered, quickly gave way and fled, many of them towards the river, but by far the greater part to their left, which was as yet unassailed. . . . [61]

The joint fire of Moore's four guns with that of the 6th, 8th, and 9th Louisiana Infantry repelled the first line of attack; but the darkness, gunsmoke, and general confusion in the Tigers' front made it increasingly difficult for the Confederates to draw a bead on subsequent Union lines following close behind.[62] The 6th Maine's second and third lines of battle, still advancing at trail arms, soon overwhelmed the defenders in both redoubts, capturing the four guns and deploying within easy rifle range of the pontoon bridge.

Shrouded by darkness and smoke, the defenders had no idea how large the attacking force was, which added to their confusion and hastened their collapse. Later, when the Confederate prisoners realized the 6th Maine alone made the initial attack, they were shocked. "We all allowed," one prisoner proclaimed, "that the whole Army of the Potomac were coming, you'uns kept up such a wicked yelling."[63]

One impetuous member of the 6th, Sergeant Otis Roberts, entered the enemy works in advance of the rest of the regiment. Realizing he was alone and surrounded, he immediately surrendered. His captivity was short lived, however, for as soon as he saw his comrades entering the works he yelled "I take it back" as he rushed for and secured the colors of the 8th Louisiana.[64] He received a Congressional Medal of Honor for distinguished valor on this day.

Many brave Louisianans met the same fate as a young Confederate artillery lieutenant. Just as he was about to pull the lanyard of a shotted piece, a Union officer demanded, "Drop that lanyard!" Refusing, the "bright, smooth-faced youth" was killed before he could fire the gun. Even the risk of death from randomly flying bullets did not deter a scavenger from promptly removing the corpse's boots.[65]

Since the chain of rifle pits to the left of the larger fort ran almost parallel to the direction of advance of the charging Federals, the members of Godwin's brigade, as well as the 5th and 7th Louisiana, could not see, let alone fire into, the charging ranks of the 6th Maine. "The conformation of the ground," one Tarheel remembered, "was such that we could not direct our fire so as to bear upon the heavy lines that were thrown against Hays, and he, after a gallant resistance, was overcome. . . ."[66] Once the redoubts fell the Confederate left flank was in serious jeopardy of being turned or encircled by the enemy.

Confederate officers unsuccessfully attempted to rally those troops who had escaped from the captured works. The area between the redoubts and the river was a mass of confusion. Frantic men crowded around the approaches to the pontoon bridge in an effort to reach the safety of the southern bank. Many of them fell victim to random Federal and Confederate shots as they milled in semi-darkness about the narrow, cleared plain seeking an opportunity to escape.

General Hays successfully rallied remnants of the 9th Louisiana and led them in a desperate counterattack on the redoubts. Together with the 6th and 57th North Carolina, led by Godwin, the Tigers were able to drive the enemy from the larger fort. The victory was short-lived, however, as the 5th Wisconsin finally reached the Confederate works and clambered into the redoubt.[67]

Fierce hand-to-hand fighting raged back and forth within the redoubts. One Union veteran remembered how both sides used "their muskets for clubs, and, when the work was too close for that, dropping their guns and pommeling with their fists."[68] A Tiger later recalled: "Our men clubbed their muskets and used them freely over Yankees heads."[69]

In the close quarters, the bayonet became a valuable weapon. "Here the unusual sight of death by bayonet wounds was witnessed," a Federal later recalled. "A dozen or more Confederate soldiers showing bayonet wounds, as well as some Union dead."[70]

The Confederates seemed to be getting the best of their outnumbered opponents when the balance of Ellmaker's brigade, the 49th and 119th Pennsylvania, scaled the earthworks.

A deadly fire poured into Ellmaker's right flank from the rifle pits on the Confederate left. General Russell, who had been wounded during the attack but remained on the field, hurriedly sent a call for Colonel Upton to advance his brigade and silence the enemy guns. Anxious to make the most of this opportunity in brigade command, the 24-year-old West Point graduate ordered the 5th Maine and 121st New York, which were already deployed less than 500 yards from the enemy line, to unsling their knapsacks and approach the Confederate works in silence to avoid enemy detection. When within 25 yards of the enemy line, the order to charge was given. Emerging from the darkness and smoke, which also covered this portion of the field, the Federals were practically in the pits before the 54th North Carolina, left by Godwin to defend the line while he led the other two Tarheel regiments against the redoubts, realized they were under attack. After a brief struggle, the surprised defenders abandoned the position.[71]

Observing how close he was to the pontoon bridge, Upton ordered several companies of the 121st New York forward to capture it, thereby blocking the enemy's main avenue of escape.

Upton also spied the flags of the 5th and 7th Louisiana flying defiantly over the rifle pits to his right. Realizing that his flank was in extreme jeopardy, the young acting brigade commander ordered Colonel Clark S. Edwards of the 5th Maine to take a detachment and attack the Tigers. Before sending his men forward, however, Upton decided to take advantage of the fact that, due to the smoke and darkness, the Tigers could not see the number of troops he had in the captured works. "When I give the command to charge," Upton yelled as loudly as he could, "move forward. If they fire upon you, I will move six lines of battle over you and bayonet every one of them." The ruse worked and large groups of Confederates, discovering the bridge was in Union control, threw down their arms and surrendered.[72]

In the midst of the hundreds of demoralized Confederate soldiers whose only interest was to find an escape from the mayhem, Colonel Godwin rallied a small number of his command and threw together a line of battle. Retreating in stages, his men resisted the advancing Union troops. General Early's official report of the battle gave a descriptive account of the valiant stand made by this officer and his stubborn band of followers:

> ... when his men had dwindled to 60 or 70, the rest having been captured, killed, wounded, or lost in the darkness, and he was completely surrounded by the enemy, who were, in fact, mixed up with his men, some one cried out that Colonel Godwin's order was for them to surrender, and he immediately called for the man who made the declaration, and threatened to blow his brains out if he could find him, declaring his purpose to fight to the last moment, and calling upon his men to stand by him. He was literally overpowered by mere force of numbers and was taken with his arms in his hands.[73]

More Union soldiers poured into the works from Upton's brigade, sealing the fate of all Confederates who had failed to escape to the southern bank. When ordered to surrender, Lieutenant Charles Pierce of the 7th Louisiana broke his sword over his knee and defiantly handed the hilt to his Yankee captor.[74]

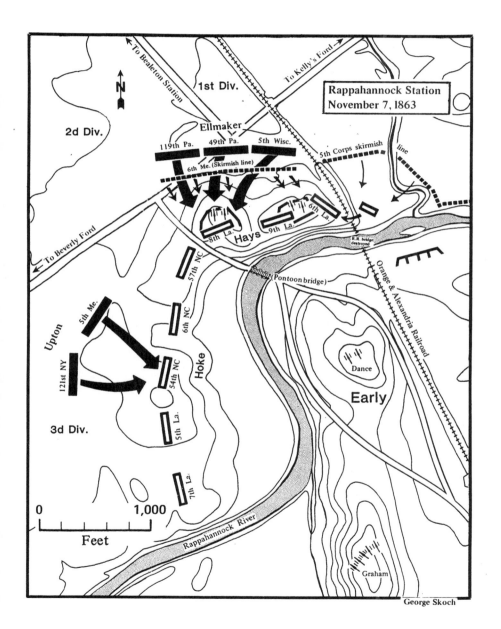

Rappahannock Station
November 7, 1863

To Bealeton Station

1st Div.

To Kelly's Ford

2d Div.

Ellmaker

119th Pa. 49th Pa. 5th Wisc.

6th Me. (Skirmish line)

5th Corps skirmish line

8th La. Hays 9th La. 6th La.

To Beverly Ford

57th NC

R.R. bridge destroyed

(Pontoon bridge)

6th NC

5th Me.

Upton

121st NY

54th NC

Hoke

5th La.

3d Div.

7th La.

Dance

Early

Orange & Alexandria Railroad

0   1,000

Feet

Rappahannock River

Graham

George Skoch

25

Although the bridgehead was now under Yankee control, many Tarheels and Tigers frantically attempted to force their way across the pontoon bridge. Most were immediately felled by enemy fire. Those not willing to risk the enemy guns at the bridge attempted to swim to the southern bank. Few escaped in this manner, however, for if the Federal fire did not stop them the freezing November waters of the Rappahannock did. Colonels Monaghan and Terry of the 6th and 7th Louisiana respectively, were among those who successfully swam to the southern bank.[75]

General Hays was one of the few defenders lucky enough to cross the pontoon bridge. While on horseback attempting to rally troops, Hays was surrounded by the enemy and forced to surrender. He could not control his horse, however, and as he tried to return his withdrawn sword to its scabbard, his mount was startled and plunged through the enemy line. Luckily for the general, the horse's path was in the direction of the pontoon bridge. The horse and rider rushed past the startled Federal defenders enabling Hays to escape unharmed but extremely shaken. Colonel Peck of the 9th Louisiana also successfully raced his horse across the bridge.[76]

Most of the Confederates, especially the Tarheels who were quickly surrounded and captured by Upton's men, were not as fortunate as Hays and his regimental commanders. Out of the original 2,000 defenders, only some 461 men escaped.[77]

Ironically, while Russell's division was overruning the Confederate position, observers on the southern bank, including Generals Lee and Early, were virtually unaware of the disaster across the river. The gathering darkness and smoke prevented close observation of the conflict, and a large portion of the battlefield was hidden from view by the height of the earthworks and intervening hillsides. Add to this an acoustical shadow caused by a strong southeasterly wind which muffled the sound of gunfire from the redoubts, and one could understand why those south of the river had no knowledge of the seriousness of the situation only a few hundred yards away.

Lee assumed that the spurts of flame he observed emanating from friendly and hostile guns were the result of either a Federal reconnaissance or an enemy feint to draw the Confederates' attention away from French at Kelly's Ford. Furthermore, he had great confidence in the defenders' ability to repulse any force thrown against them. Not only were two of his best brigades well-entrenched in redoubts and rifle pits, but both flanks rested solidly on the river. The enemy could not advance a line any longer than the length of the works.

The sun having set, Lee also believed that Meade would not storm the works that night since the confusion created by the darkness was often as great for attackers as defenders. Satisfied that the situation at

Rappahannock Station had stabilized for the evening, Lee retired to his headquarters to finalize plans for the attack on French's force the next morning.[78]

It was only after the commanding general had departed that Early gradually began to realize what had occurred across the river. His first indication of trouble came from a member of his staff, Major Samuel Hale. Upon returning from the northern bank, Hale brought word that, although he had not personally observed Federal troops in the works, he had been told by two of Hays' men that some Confederates had been driven from the line.

Giving little credence to this report, Early sent another member of his staff, Major John W. Daniel, to evaluate the situation along the northern bank. In case the rumor was true, however, the ever-cautious 47-year-old division commander, also a West Point graduate, took the precaution of sending Brigadier General John Pegram's Brigade to the southern end of the bridge to stop the enemy from crossing it.

Later, as Early headed toward the bridge to take charge of the situation personally, he met Major Daniel bearing grim news. Hays, who had barely escaped himself, Daniel reported, had told him that the greater portion of Hays' brigade had been captured and that Godwin's troops were cut off from the bridge.

Shaken by this news, Early stood helplessly on the southern bank. "I had the mortification to hear the final struggle of these devoted men and to be made painfully aware of their capture, without the possibility of being able to go to their relief."[79] Deciding it would be folly to send any more men across the bridge, Early strengthened the defensive position south of the river. He also ordered Dance and Graham, whose guns had been of little help to their comrades across the river and were utterly useless now due to the close proximity of the two lines, to train their pieces on the bridge in case the enemy should attempt to force a passage.

After waiting an ample amount of time to give everyone who could an opportunity to escape across the bridge, Early ordered the southern end of it burned. Thirteen volunteers, commanded by Captain Sam Buck of the 13th Virginia, agreed to attempt this dangerous mission.

With enemy troops less than 50 yards away, Buck crawled through the darkness to the bridge. Quickly placing hay and other combustibles in every crevice he could reach, Buck lit the material and proceeded to run up the bank to the Confederate works. Having accomplished their mission without any casualties, Buck and his detachment watched as "the burning mass floated down the river."[80]

The losses suffered by Early's division at Rappahannock Station and Rodes' at Kelly's Ford were very costly to the Confederate cause. Louis

Philippe d'Orleans, more popularly known as the Comte de Paris, a French nobleman who wrote a popular history of the war, later observed that these losses were "the most painful which had as yet been inflicted on [Lee's] army."[81] At the ford Lee lost almost 360 men and at the station he lost 1,672.[82] More than 2,000 irreplaceable seasoned veterans were gone — a staggering loss, especially coming on the heels of the Confederate casualties at Gettysburg and Bristoe Station.

While engaging a comparable number of troops, the Federals achieved their brilliant victories with significantly fewer casualties: 42 at Kelly's Ford and 419 at Rappahannock Station. Union troops also captured seven Confederate flags and the four guns of the Louisiana Guard Artillery.[83]

Many of the officers and men of the Army of Northern Virginia were more shaken by the double defeats of November 7 than by any other setback yet experienced in the war. Lee's assistant adjutant general, Colonel Walter H. Taylor, felt that this episode was "the saddest chapter in the history of this army."[84] Another officer expressed more succinctly the opinion of the army as a whole: "It is absolutely sickening, and I feel personally disgraced by the issue of the late campaign, as does every one in the command. Oh, how every day is proving the value of General Jackson to us!"[85]

Lee and his subordinates advanced a number of reasons for the demoralizing reverses. In his official report Early cited the weakness of the defenses, lack of more than one bridge, insufficient artillery support, darkness, and high winds for the defeat at Rappahannock Station. He also falsely assumed that the Union force actually participating in the attack at the station consisted of two entire corps when in truth it was only two brigades.[86]

Another Confederate officer claimed that the Federal foot soldiers had been stimulated by whiskey to increase their courage.[87]

In Lee's official report he found no fault with his men "as the courage and good conduct of the troops engaged have been too often tried to admit of question." Instead he was critical, without censoring any individual officers, of the way his men were handled in the two affairs. One example he cited was the impulsive charge of the 30th North Carolina during the Union attack at the ford.[88] Neither he nor his subordinates, however, expressed what was probably the primary cause for the defeats — the ability of the Union army and its commander to carry out a successful tactical strike.

While the Confederates searched for reasons for their failure at Kelly's Ford and Rappahannock Station, the Federal cause received a much needed boost from this offensive success on Virginia soil. An officer on Sedgwick's staff noted soon after the actions: "I am going to 'blow' a little

... for it was, I believe, the most, if not the only, decided success in which I have participated in the War."[89]

The victories came at a time when Meade's credibility as an army commander had reached an all-time low. "The operation being successful," the Federal commander wrote to his wife two days later, "the army is in fine spirits, and of course I am more popular than ever, having been greeted yesterday as I rode through the ranks with great cheering."[90] Meade even received congratulations from a source who had not yet publicly acknowledged his success at Gettysburg, President Lincoln. "I have seen your dispatches about operations on the Rappahannock on Saturday," Lincoln wired Meade, "and I wish to say, 'Well done.' "[91]

Even the enemy praised the Union success. One Confederate officer declared that the Federal charge at Rappahannock Station was "the most brilliant feat of arms he had yet seen."[92]

Lee attempted to take these defeats in stride. When addressing General Hays a few days later he asked his brigade commander:

"General, this is a sad affair. How do you feel today?"

"I feel, sir, as well as a man can feel who has lost so many men."

"That is all over now and cannot be helped. The only thing is to try to get even with them today."[93]

Since the beginning of his Bristoe Campaign, less than one month earlier, Lee had lost more than 4,000 men while inflicting fewer than 1,000 Union casualties. The Confederate commander could only hope that good fortune would once again smile on his troops. Little did he realize, however, that these latest setbacks marked a significant turning point for his dwindling command. November 7, 1863, was the last day his army as a whole would ever have the offensive capability to reach, let alone cross, the upper Rappahannock River.

CHAPTER II

"The Promise of Brilliant Success"

The Confederate commander left General Early at Rappahannock Station on the evening of November 7 as darkness began to mask the activity across the river. Lee rode back to his headquarters at Brandy Station satisfied with the security of the bridgehead and confident about the prospects of the following morning. A rare opportunity presented itself to the Army of Northern Virginia. While only two brigades held a large portion of Meade's forces in check north of the river at Rappahannock Station, Lee planned to strike the Union troops deployed along the southern bank with the majority of his army.

Lee and his staff had already arrived at headquarters when a courier galloped into camp with an urgent dispatch from General Early. The bridgehead at Rappahannock Station, his irascible division commander announced in the note, had fallen.[1]

Lee was shocked by this dismal news, for he had had no warning that the position was even in jeopardy. Not only had he just lost the majority of two of his finest brigades, but the loss of his bridgehead meant that his Rappahannock line was no longer secure. Without the threat of a Confederate flanking movement north of the river, Meade could now throw his entire force across Kelly's Ford without concern for the security of his line of communication.

This development placed Lee in a posture he abhorred, but one to which his troops were becoming all too accustomed. Instead of the anticipated attack at Kelly's Ford, the aggressive Confederate commander was now forced to withdraw his army to a defensive position southwest of the river.

Unfortunately, the relatively flat and extensively cleared plain between the Rappahannock and Rapidan rivers did not favor a strong defensive position. No matter where Lee formed his line, either flank would be susceptible to a turning movement, an especially dangerous situation with the Rapidan at his rear.

Lee ruled out the possibility of a forced march of more than twenty miles to his previously established Rapidan line due to the close proximity of the enemy and the subsequent risk of exposing his trains to capture. Perhaps the most significant reason for Lee's desire to remain north of the Rapidan, however, was the fact that it was not in his nature to surrender such a large portion of his beloved Virginia, even a section that was practically barren due to two and a half years of active campaigning and occupation, to Federal control without at least a show of force.

Lee decided on an area between Brandy Station and Culpeper Court House for his makeshift line of defense. His right flank would be anchored on Pony Mountain, about two and a half miles southeast of Culpeper, and would extend about five miles to the north, blocking the Federal approaches to the town.

Soon after midnight, regimental commanders began to rouse their men with orders to break camp. The news surprised those weary foot soldiers who were yet unaware of the developments along the Rappahannock. Anticipating that they had experienced the last of active campaigning for the year, many had started to build permanent shelters. One Confederate later recalled that all their "calculations about winter quarters were knocked in the head for the time. Some of the men had completed nice cabins and expected to move into them the next morning, but such is war."[2]

It never took Lee's army long to break camp. As Carlton McCarthy recorded in his reflections on life in the Army of Northern Virginia, in addition to his rifle, caps, and cartridges, "the private soldier consisted of one man, one hat, one jacket, one shirt, one pair of pants, one pair of drawers, one pair of shoes, and one pair of socks. His baggage was one blanket, one rubber blanket, and one haversack." Any additional accouterments accumulated during the respite were left behind for the next occupants of the camp.[3]

Throughout the early morning chill of November 8, Lee's army quickly withdrew to its new defensive position north of Culpeper, where Confederate staff officers carefully positioned the troops and artillery as they arrived. In his diary, Captain Robert E. Park of the 12th Alabama Infantry recorded that once his regiment was initially assigned a place in line, the men "began to throw up breastworks as a protection against shell in case of attack, in two different places, using our tin cups, tin plates and bayonets, in place of spades and picks, of which we had none."[4] Hill's corps was assigned to defend the Confederate left flank and Ewell's the right.

Although Lee's men began their withdrawal shortly after midnight, dawn still caught some of them falling back from the enemy's front. Fearful that a Federal attack could come at any time, Confederate officers did their best to hurry their tardy troops into the new position. They had nothing to fear, however, since the cautious Meade was slow to push his victorious troops from their bridgehead south of the Rappahannock.

Throughout the evening of November 7, Federal troops quickly

31

crossed the Rappahannock River on pontoon bridges near Kelly's Ford and hurried into position a short distance from the enemy line. General French, the left wing commander, and his staff spent the night anxiously gathering as much information as possible about the disposition of Confederate troops in their front from runaway slaves, enemy deserters, and reconnaissance missions. The intelligence gained from these sources led French to believe that Lee intended to attack his isolated force at dawn.

Meanwhile, Sedgwick attempted to discover what he could about the disposition of enemy troops across the Rappahannock from the captured redoubts. Following the burning of the pontoon bridge by Early's men, and the cessation of fighting along the northern bank, an uneasy silence fell upon the area, broken only by occasional picket shots.

The sketchy reports of his wing commanders left Meade in the dark about Lee's intentions. Still fearing the threat of an enemy attack on French's force, Meade at 11:30 p.m. on November 7 instructed Sedgwick to send the V Corps and two brigades of the VI to Kelly's Ford to reinforce French. He also ordered his right wing commander to demonstrate against the enemy across the river at daylight and, if possible, throw down a pontoon bridge and cross to the opposite bank.

Meade instructed French to advance at dawn along the southern bank in the direction of Rappahannock Station, to drive the enemy from Sedgwick's front, and to assist the VI Corps in crossing the river. The Federal commander would rest much more comfortably once his army was united south of the river.[5]

At 4:00 a.m., Brigadier General Joseph B. Carr, commanding the 3rd Division, III Corps, sent two regiments forward to reconnoiter the Confederate position. They had advanced about one and a half miles southwest of the Federal line when they discovered an abandoned enemy camp. Carr immediately dispatched the remainder of the brigade forward in an attempt to locate the camp's former occupants.

The troops sent ahead by Carr were commanded by Colonel J. Warren Keifer. They encountered the Confederate rear guard — cavalry and horse artillery — on a hill adjacent to the Orange and Alexandria Railroad, about two and a half miles from Brandy Station. Deploying his infantry and one battery of artillery, Keifer quickly drove the enemy from the hill and pursued them to Brandy Station, where he was ordered to halt by General Carr.[6]

While Keifer's men were driving the Confederates beyond the station, Sedgwick was still uncertain whether or not the enemy was entrenched across the river. As Meade stated in a dispatch to Halleck that evening, "The morning was so smoky and hazy, it was impossible to ascertain at Rappahannock Station the position of the enemy, and it was not till the arrival of the column from Kelly's Ford it was definitely known the position at Rappahanock Station was evacuated."[7]

By the time the pontoon bridge was laid across the river and the men of the VI Corps joined with the III in pursuit of the retreating Confederates, Lee's troops were already well established in their new position southwest of Brandy Station. It was late afternoon before the two Yankee corps advanced, practically unmolested, to the station, where they halted to await further orders from General Meade.

For many Union soldiers the most memorable moment of the day was the sight of the III and VI Corps meeting on the open, rolling plain northeast of Brandy Station and marching together in line of battle along the Orange and Alexandria Railroad. Years later, Colonel Regis de Trobriand, whose troops had driven the enemy from Kelly's Ford the day before, described the scene in his memoirs:

> The pursuit began immediately in order of battle. The country was admirably fitted for it. It is almost the only part of Virginia where the open land extends to any distance without obstacles. So that this grand military deployment offered one of the finest spectacles which could be imagined. Let one picture to himself two army corps marching on the centre, in line of battle, in mass, the artillery in the intervals and on the roads, the flanks covered by two divisions in column, the skirmishers in advance, the cavalry on the two wings; the reserves covering the wagons in the rear; and all this mass of humanity in perfect order, rising or falling gradually according to the undulations of the plain, with the noise of the cannon, which did not cease throwing projectiles on the rearguard of the Confederates in retreat. Such was the moving picture which was given us to enjoy during that whole afternoon.[8]

While the troops reveled in the victories of the day before and the pageantry of the leisurely pursuit of the enemy across the Brandy Station plain, Meade and his staff restlessly waited north of the river on the bluff overlooking Kelly's Ford, straining to hear the familiar sounds of battle. Once he learned of the Confederate retreat, the Federal commander sent his cavalry to determine Lee's movements. He was naturally concerned about any tricks his cunning adversary might have in store for the advancing Union army.

At about 2:00 p.m., Meade and his staff finally crossed the Rappahannock to learn first hand the situation at the front.[9] While riding to Brandy Station, they passed the V Corps deployed near the ford and the II Corps a little farther from the river. When they encountered Major General Gouverneur K. Warren, the 33-year-old II Corps commander, Colonel Lyman stated that he looked "like a man of disappointed hopes, as he gazed round the country and said, 'There's nobody [Confederates] here — nobody!' "[10]

It wasn't until late afternoon that Meade finally reached the bottleneck at Brandy Station, too late to initiate an assault on the Confederate position outside Culpeper. As the men settled into camp for the evening, it was hoped that the day's delays only postponed what some believed to be the inevitable engagement which could ultimately spell the end of this conflict. Several corps and division commanders, however, were discouraged that Lee once again was allowed to escape from a very dangerous situation — practically untouched.

Throughout November 8 there were at least six separate skirmishes between the contesting armies, principally cavalry, but the initial delays in crossing the Rappahannock and pressing south in pursuit of the enemy prevented Meade from taking full advantage of the previous day's success.[11]

Sensing that the Federal army had lost a rare opportunity to strike a critical blow to the enemy cause, greater discontent surfaced among Meade's subordinates when it was learned that Lee's troops had crossed the Rapidan River during the early morning hours of the 9th. That evening General Marsena Patrick, the Army of the Potomac's provost marshal general, wrote the following in his diary: "I think every body in this Army, or at these Head Quarters, perhaps, is disgusted tonight. . . ."[12]

To many Union officers, the situation along the Rappahannock and Rapidan rivers was too reminiscent of the aftermath of the Battle of Gettysburg, when Meade's timid pursuit of Lee's defeated army allowed the Confederates to slip relatively unscatched back into Virginia and safety. The discontent within the officer corps over Meade's inability to follow up the victories of November 7 publicly surfaced the following February and March during testimony before the U.S. Congressional Joint Committee on the Conduct of the War. The committee, under the leadership of radical Republicans, attempted to replace General Meade as the commander of the Army of the Potomac, citing certain deficiencies as a military leader.[13] Although they were unsuccessful, sufficient testimony was gathered from subordinate generals to demonstrate the dissatisfaction that existed in military ranks with Meade's ability to stand up effectively to Lee.

Major General David B. Birney, commanding the 1st Division, III Corps, testified that a timely pursuit of the enemy on November 8 could have met with great success.

At daylight I advanced, but before I reached the railroad I received orders from General Meade not to advance beyond it. . . .

... I am of the opinion that if I had been permitted to advance, as my troops were in fine condition and eager to do so, we could have struck the enemy a very severe blow.[14]

In other testimony before the committee, General Warren, the II Corps commander, also expressed disappointment over the lost opportunity:

But the whole of November 8 was almost wasted in useless and uncertain movements. I do not know who is to blame for that. But if we had advanced that day rapidly towards either Culpeper or through Stevensburg, towards the south of it, we should most certainly have cut Lee's army in two.[15]

No matter who or what was ultimately at fault for the delays of the 8th while Lee waited for the Union army to strike his makeshift line outside Culpeper, Meade's force failed to duplicate the same offensive spirit that had caught Lee off guard at Rappahannock Station and Kelly's Ford.

Realizing that an attempt by Meade to turn his exposed flanks could lead to disastrous consequences, Lee decided to retire his army during the night of November 8 to a much stronger line south of the Rapidan. His trains had been crossing the river throughout the day, so there was little congestion on the roadways as his men marched through Culpeper toward the Rapidan fords.

The weather took a turn for the worse on the 8th when cold, bitter winds brought snow to the area. Although the average soldier of both armies had been hardened by foul-weather campaigning for almost two and a half years, fording bone-chilling waters continued to rank among the most dreaded of tasks they could be called on to perform. One member of the 21st Virginia Infantry recalled, a half century later, the experience of crossing the knee-deep Rapidan that November evening:

It was the coldest water I ever forded. Oh, how cold! I can feel it now ... it was so cold it felt as if a knife had taken one's foot off; and at each step the depth of the water increased. This feeling continued until we reached the middle of the river, where the water came to the knee, and one felt as if the leg was off from the knee down. Reaching the shore and halting to put on shoes and let pants down, many of the men were so cold they could not do it.[16]

One member of the 12th Virginia Infantry remembered how "*walking was fatiguing,* and *resting was freezing.*"[17]

With the same resilience they demonstrated in the face of many other hardships, Lee's men pushed on and returned to the camps along the Rapidan which they had abandoned only a month earlier at the start of the Bristoe Campaign.

The Confederate line ran along the Rapidan for about eighteen miles, southwest from Morton's Ford. As protection for his right flank, Lee refused his line four miles from the river near Morton's Ford to Bartlett's Mill, located on the bank of Mine Run, a narrow stream that empties into the Rapidan. This little-known creek would soon become the focal point of the developing campaign.

Lee's left flank rested at Liberty Mills, a popular crossing point of the Rapidan about five and a half miles southwest of Orange Court House. Ewell's corps, under the temporary command of General Early due to Ewell's lingering complications following the amputation of his leg more than a year earlier, occupied roughly half the line on the right while Hill's corps manned the Confederate left. Cavalry covered both flanks as well as the fords along the lower Rapidan.

Both the Orange Turnpike and the Orange Plank Road ran from east to west, south of and roughly parallel to the Confederate line, providing Lee with two good roads on which to shift his troops quickly from flank to flank if necessary. To effectively monitor and orchestrate the deployment of his force, the Confederate commander established his headquarters on the side of Clark's Mountain at the center of his line.[18]

With a secure position south of the Rapidan River and a watchful eye on the Federals in the hope of anticipating Meade's next move, Lee's immediate attention turned to supplying the daily needs of his army. Commissary problems never were far from his thoughts at anytime during the war, but Lee was especially sensitive to supply shortages as the conflict entered its third winter.

The twin Confederate failures of Lee's Gettysburg Campaign and the fall of Vicksburg, Mississippi, both within the same gloomy week the previous July, strained the army's already meager commissary to the breaking point. The Army of Northern Virginia never enjoyed the bounties of food that might have come from the rich Pennsylvania farmlands if the northern invasion had been successful; while the Federal blockade of the Mississippi River, following the Confederate surrender at Vicksburg, brought an abrupt halt to the flow of vital food stuffs — cattle, especially — from the trans-Mississippi region.

The supply shortages had an immediate and irreversible impact on Lee's army and on the Confederacy in general. Stock piles shrank, military and civilian rations were cut, and disgruntled Confederate soldiers deserted from the army in ever-increasing numbers. Unfortunately for the Southern cause, there was no improvement in the dismal situation within sight. For the coming winter, Confederate commissary general, Colonel Lucius B. Northrop, estimated that his department would butcher 4,000 head of cattle — the previous winter his butchers had processed 40,000 head.[19]

In addition to the shortages of food for his army, it was all too evident to Lee, with winter approaching, that there were also insufficient amounts of shoes and warm clothing for his men. There was also a dangerous shortage of corn for the army's mules and horses. As with the plains north of the Rapidan and Rappahannock rivers, the months of active campaigning had virtually stripped the land south of the Rapidan of animal forage.

On November 10, Lee sent an urgent dispatch to Secretary of War James A. Seddon requesting that he do everything in his power to see that these items were forwarded to the army as soon as possible. Two days later, in another dispatch to Seddon, Lee threatened to fall back to the defenses of Richmond if the railway system was not repaired so that the commissary department could improve the flow of supplies to the army.[20]

Despite Lee's threat to withdraw to Richmond, the Army of Northern Virginia remained on the Rapidan, picketing the fords and monitoring the activity of the enemy. This respite along the river was not totally uneventful. Three men were executed for desertion by a firing squad, witnessed by six brigades of Ewell's corps. Such demonstrations of discipline had the desired effect on the troops present. Following this particular execution one Virginian observed, "if I live a thousand years, I will never be willing to see another."[21]

Also during this break in campaigning, Lee was given a rather unusual gift by the City Council of Richmond for his valuable service to the Confederacy. The council presented him with a house. Lee declined the generous offer, however, since his family had no need for it. Instead, he requested that the council use the money to provide in some way for the "relief of the families of our soldiers in the field, who are more in want of assistance, and more deserving it, than myself. . . ."[22]

Even though the Confederate commander spent a great deal of his time enforcing discipline and providing for the needs of his men, he always kept a watchful eye on the activities of his adversary north of the Rapidan. On November 12, Lee wired President Jefferson Davis that reports led him to believe that Meade was preparing to strike across the river. Demonstrating once again an uncanny ability almost to read his opponent's mind, a skill Lee seemed to possess over each of the previous commanders of the Army of the Potomac, he came close to predicting Meade's next move, two weeks before it began. "There are indications . . . ," he informed the President, "that this advance will take place on our right by the lower fords, Germanna and Ely's, as if with the intention of striking for the Richmond and Fredericksburg Railroad." He also took the opportunity to emphasize to the President that unless something was done to replenish the army's dwindling supplies, he could not ensure victory.[23]

On November 24, President Davis visited Lee and his army to evaluate the situation for himself. During his two-day stay, Davis and Lee most likely discussed the issue of supply shortages and other matters affecting the defense of the Rapidan line. The visit was also marked by a Presidential review of both Ewell's and Hill's corps, always a grand occasion for the men in the ranks.[24] Once Davis left the front, attention turned to enemy activities north of the river.

While Lee pressured his superiors to prepare his army adequately for a possible Federal advance, the opposite was true in the Yankee camp. In what was becoming an all-too-familiar occurrence, Meade's superiors continued their attempt to spur their general forward.

Once Meade learned that Lee had fallen back across the Rapidan, he decided to suspend the pursuit while his engineers rebuilt the Orange and Alexandria Railroad to Brandy Station. He could then replenish his supplies while he pondered his next move.

Meanwhile, the troops were ordered to establish camps on the plains around Brandy Station. Many units settled at sites they had occupied only a month earlier. The difference, however, was that in their absence the Confederates had begun to prepare for what they had thought would be their own winter camp. "Whole villages of quite sizable houses were half finished," one Union observer noted in his journal, "and thousands of shingles split out for roofing. . . ."[25]

Not only had the Confederates constructed huts which were quickly pressed into service by the Federals, they had also begun to corduroy roads in preparation for the coming winter storms.[26] The Union army gratefully utilized the materials and improvements so conveniently left behind by its enemy.

With the Confederates solidly entrenched below the Rapidan, the Federals settled into camp between Culpeper and Brandy Station. As work progressed on the railroad, Meade had an important decision to make. Should he establish winter quarters or continue his push south?

The excitement generated in Washington by the Union victories of November 7 was quickly tempered by the news that Meade had allowed Lee to escape across the Rapidan. One of the Union general's greatest critics, Secretary of War Edwin M. Stanton, was especially angered by this latest offensive lapse. Stanton's discontent with Meade's timid performance became all too evident on November 11 when the secretary refused to receive an honor guard carrying the enemy colors captured at Rappahannock Station. What made the rebuff an even greater snub to the whole Army of the Potomac was that the guard was led by the slightly wounded hero of Rappahannock Station, General Russell.[27]

Realizing that a decision to suspend campaigning for the winter could result in the end of his tenure as commander of the Army of the Potomac, Meade decided to consult with his superiors concerning his next move. On November 13, he wired the capital with a request to meet with Halleck and Stanton in Washington the next day. Halleck quickly agreed to the meeting.[28]

At 6:00 a.m. on the 14th of November, Meade and three aides set out on horseback for the eight mile journey between army headquarters near Brandy Station and Bealeton, where they were to catch a military train for Washington. In Meade's absence, General Sedgwick, as the ranking major general, commanded the army.[29]

Meade's trip to the capital, however, was not destined to become a respite from the constant vigilance he had learned was necessary when opposing Lee. At 1:00 a.m. on the 15th, Meade received a dispatch from his Chief of Staff, General Humphreys, stating that three runaway slaves and a Confederate deserter brought word that the enemy was abandoning its line along the Rapidan. He informed Meade that cavalry patrols had been sent out to check the rumor and assured his commander that "our left as well as our right has been looked after."[30]

Meade spent some anxious hours in the capital awaiting further word from his chief of staff. Concern over a possible Confederate advance, perhaps Lee's second attempt within a month of a flanking movement, was foremost on the commander's mind. Throughout the afternoon and early evening of the 15th, Humphreys kept Meade updated as reports came into headquarters from various cavalry patrols. It was not until 7:45 p.m. that he was able to assure the absent commander that the enemy was not on the move, but still held its line along the Rapidan.

Buried in two of the dispatches Humphreys sent Meade on the 15th was perhaps the most heartening news of the day. "Railroad bridge at Rappahannock Station just reported finished," he wired. "The track to that point will be laid to-day."[31] It would not be long before the lifeline of his army would once again be functioning.

During Meade's absence Sedgwick permitted subordinates to arrange a punch party, a diversion their dour commander never would have permitted, especially while the army was still actively campaigning. Of the same mettle as Meade, Colonel Lyman was highly critical of the affair. "But mice play when the cat is too good natured. . . ," Lyman recorded in his journal. "Active operations would highly benefit the army; for whiskey drinking is taken to as a defense against nothing to do."[32]

Many officers felt entitled to such distractions as this punch party because they felt Meade was too aloof from the needs of his officers and enlisted men. General Patrick observed that the general "seems to know little about his Army. He disgusts by his Apathy and indifference as regards his Troops . . . ."[33] Many subordinates would have been happier if Meade had been compelled to remain in Washington permanently.

Meade did return to his headquarters, however, in the early afternoon of November 16. If his council with the general-in-chief and secretary of war had produced an offensive plan, Meade did not reveal it to his staff.[34] It is more likely that Meade had been given general orders to continue the offensive against the enemy in whatever manner he saw fit, the only restriction being that his operations must continue along his present line of communication.[35]

By November 20, Meade had ruled out as impractical a direct assault against any portion of the Confederate position or a movement around the enemy left flank. Lee was strengthening his line daily and his left flank was at least twice as far from the Federal base at Brandy Station as his right. A Federal movement around the enemy left would not only be time consuming, but would also uncover Meade's line of communications with Washington.[36]

Following his return from Washington, the Union commander gained two important pieces of information from Confederate deserters, prisoners, and Federal scouts. Meade was quick to realize that the new information could provide him with the offensive advantage he so desperately sought. The knowledge that Lee had left the lower fords of the Rapidan virtually unguarded seemed to invite a Union advance. Even more significant was the intelligence that the Orange Plank Road and the Orange Turnpike, both of which ran behind the Confederate line, were essentially devoid of obstructions. With a sudden advance across the Rapidan, the Federal army could gain access to the enemy's rear practically unmolested. If this information were true, it pointed out a very serious oversight by the usually thorough Confederate commander.

Sources also informed Meade of the positions of both enemy corps and their relative strengths. Estimates placed about 50,000 Confederate troops behind the fortifications confronted by a Yankee force in excess of 80,000.[37] The reported enemy strength proved to be unusually accurate, considering Union army intelligence's penchant for exaggeration and overestimation.

Trusting that his sources' information was accurate, Meade decided to turn the enemy right flank in a maneuver similar to that which Major General Joseph Hooker had attempted in his Chancellorsville Campaign six months earlier. In his official report, Meade summarized the strategy:

The plan I decided on was to cross the Rapidan at the lower

fords, in three columns, and by a prompt movement seize the plank road and turnpike, advancing rapidly toward Orange Court-House, thus turning the enemy's works, and compelling him to give battle on ground not previously selected or prepared, and I indulged the hope that in the execution of this plan I should be enabled to fall on part of the enemy's forces before he could effect a concentration, and thus so cripple him as to render more certain the success of the final struggle.[38]

The success or failure of the plan, Meade realized, depended on the element of surprise. He was therefore careful to keep his jump-off date, November 24, a secret from all but his closest confidants. Meade hoped to steal a march on Lee, and, by the 25th, plant his force on a strong position along the high ground south of the Confederate line and west of Mine Run.

The plan for the 24th called for General Warren's II Corps to cross the Rapidan at Germanna Ford and proceed to Robinson's (also known as Robertson's) Tavern, located at the important Locust Grove crossroads on the Turnpike, four miles southeast of the Confederate right flank. French's III Corps was to cover the Federal right flank by crossing the Rapidan at Jacob's Ford, three and a half miles up river from Germanna Ford, and proceeding over back roads — actually no more than paths through dense wilderness — to connect with Warren's right flank north of the tavern. Since the III Corps would be moving relatively close to and in front of a portion of the enemy line, making it vulnerable to attack, Meade decided to have Sedgwick's VI Corps follow and support French. These two corps were the largest in the army, together comprising almost half of the Federal force.

The V and I Corps, under Major Generals George Sykes and John Newton, were to cross the Rapidan at Culpeper Mine Ford, four and a half miles down river from Germanna Ford, and proceed down the Plank Road to the crossroads at Parker's Store. At this point, the V Corps would continue west on the Plank Road to New Hope Church. Meanwhile, the I Corps was to move northwest from Parker's Store, plugging the gap between Warren's left flank and Sykes' right.

David Gregg's cavalry division would cover the Federal left flank. A small detachment would accompany French's column while the remaining cavalry units would guard fords and the Federal wagon train.[39]

Meade called all five of his corps commanders to his headquarters on the evening of November 23 to issue the marching orders for the next morning. In an effort to reduce the possibility of confusion and error, he gave sketches of the routes of march to each subordinate. Meade told the generals to issue ten days' rations and instructed them to have only essential wagons — ambulances and those carrying ammunition and other necessary supplies — accompany their columns to facilitate the advance.[40]

The Union high command had considerable confidence in Meade's plan. "[It] promised brilliant success," Humphreys later recalled; "to insure it required prompt, vigorous action, and intelligent compliance with the programme on the part of corps and other subordinate commanders."[41] Unfortunately for the Federal effort, however, things began to go wrong from the beginning.

Private Wilbur Fisk of the 2nd Vermont Infantry graphically described, in a letter home, the events of the morning of November 24:

> ... we had orders to be ready to march at an early hour. Accordingly, at precisely three o'clock in the morning, our quiet dreams were broken up by the rattling of drums all through camp, and forthwith we commenced to break up housekeeping — for the most of us had built us tip top houses — and to prepare for another campaign or for whatever was to be accomplished. The weather was grim and forbidding, and the rain drops as they came pattering on our tent that morning, driven by a regular nor'easter, had a very dismal sound in view of the prospect before us. A rainstorm is a very uninviting auxiliary with which to commence a long campaign at any season of the year, but more especially now when cold weather has come and when wet clothes can hardly be made to suggest anything but discomforts of the least desirable kind. Our tents become wet and heavy, and to carry these in our knapsacks with all the rest of the clothing that we are obliged to carry at this time of the year, was going to make a pretty heavy draft upon the strength of a fellow's back bone. It is the last straw that breaks the camel's back, and the addition of a few extra pounds of water might have the same effect on us, for our packs have hitherto been as heavy as seemed possible for us to carry.[42]

In addition to making conditions difficult for the foot soldier, the heavy rain also caused swollen rivers and streams and turned the rough country roads into bottomless quagmires, making Humphreys' "prompt, vigorous action" impossible. Although he realized that any delay could place the success of his offensive in serious jeopardy, Meade had no choice but to postpone the advance.[43] This decision came as welcome news to the men in the ranks. "You may judge of our satisfaction then," Fisk continued in his letter, "when we heard that the order to march had been postponed for two days."[44]

Meade was not happy with this development. He realized that any delay risked the element of surprise upon which the success of the movement so greatly depended. The Federal commander reluctantly decided to resume the offensive on Thursday, November 26, Thanksgiving Day. He could only hope that Lee had not learned of the aborted advance.

That same night a Confederate scout from Culpeper reached Lee's headquarters with news of Meade's intended advance. Lee wired the report to Davis early on the 25th.

> ... the First Army Corps of General Meade's army, encamped near the court-house, had been provided with eight days' rations and received marching orders, their destination unknown, but their own men reported they were to move forward .... From these reports and the indications in the Washington papers, I infer that General Meade intends to advance.[45]

Lee immediately placed his troops on alert to march at a moment's notice. With two good highways at his disposal — the Plank Road and the Turnpike — Lee was confident that he could quickly strike Meade's column once the Federals crossed the Rapidan.

Now with both Lee's and Meade's troops poised for action, it was just a matter of time before this latest and, for both commanders perhaps the most frustrating episode of the war in the East, was to begin.

CHAPTER III
"The Enemy Was Throwing Minie-Balls. . .
by the Bucket-Full"

A Federal general and his staff slowly rode down the dirt path, their horses' progress hampered by the long line of infantrymen crowded into the narrow trail, roughly cut through the dense forest. Finally reaching the northern bank of the Rapidan River, near Jacob's Ford, Brigadier General Henry Prince, commanding the 2nd Division of the III Corps, concealed himself in the fringe of the woods bordering the river and carefully studied the terrain and enemy dispositions along the opposite bank. It was about noon, November 26, 1863.

Since his division was the vanguard of the Federal right wing, composed of the III and VI Corps, the responsibility to push across the river and drive the enemy from the southern bank fell on Prince's troops. Being unfamiliar with the ford, the 52-year-old general decided to reconnoiter personally and supervise the crossing. His careful examination of the opposite bank led him to believe that this would be more than just a routine maneuver.

Prince discovered enemy cavalry deployed along a steep ridge about one hundred feet above the river, and what appeared to be infantry concealed in thick woods a short distance from the bank. A Union signal officer also claimed to have sighted a section of Confederate artillery nearby.

The fact that the Rapidan was swollen by recent heavy rain only added to Prince's concern. Its current and depth prohibited fording, thereby ruling out the possibility of a full-scale assault on the enemy position.[1] Prince ordered his officers to keep their men concealed from enemy observation while he personally deployed his artillery and infantry along the northern bank as cover for the assaulting force.

While Prince prepared for the attempted crossing, his corps commander, Major General William H. French, arrived on the scene. Concerned that Prince's division was already more than an hour behind schedule due to a late start and extremely slow march, French wished to expedite the crossing. Apprised by his division commander of the situation across the Rapidan, French assisted Prince in deploying artillery and hurrying the pontoon train to the front — not an easy task with the narrow, muddy road leading to the ford clogged with waiting troops.[2]

44

Once the boats reached the front, a detachment of 25 men led by Colonel Robert McAllister of the 11th New Jersey, scrambled aboard and began a mad dash across the river. To their surprise, they met little opposition and quickly dispersed the small band of Confederate cavalry picketing the southern bank. Contrary to Prince's observations, there was no enemy infantry or artillery present.[3]

With the southern side of the river now secure, Prince's engineers began constructing the pontoon bridge. It wasn't long, however, before they discovered that they would fall at least one pontoon short of reaching the opposite bank due to the swollen condition of the Rapidan. A trestle had to be constructed to complete the span, causing further delay. It was not until 4:00 p.m., well behind the schedule so carefully planned by Meade, that the balance of Prince's troops were finally able to cross.[4]

Throughout the morning and early afternoon of the 26th, Meade cooled his heels at Germanna Ford, closely monitoring French's progress in crossing the Rapidan. The Federal commander was troubled by this delay on his right flank.

In contrast to French's slow start, the head of Gouverneur Warren's II Corps had reached Germanna Ford at about 9:30 a.m. and George Sykes' V Corps had arrived at Culpeper Mine Ford at about 10:30 a.m., both well ahead of the III's noon arrival at Jacob's Ford. Although anxious to cross the river and push for the day's objective — Robinson's Tavern on the Orange Turnpike — Meade suspended the advance by the II and V Corps until the III reached and began to cross the river. Not knowing what, if any, surprises Lee might have in store for the Army of the Potomac south of the Rapidan, the Federal commander did not wish to jeopardize the safety of either Warren's or Sykes' corps. Prior to Meade's order one division of the V Corps had already crossed, but Sykes halted any further movement.[5]

After he learned that the III Corps had finally arrived on the Rapidan, Meade, well aware of the distances his corps had yet to travel that afternoon to reach the area of the tavern, sent the following dispatch to French through his chief of staff, General Humphreys:

> . . . [Meade] directs that you throw your bridge immediately, and cross without delay. I am also directed to say that your delay in reaching the river has retarded the operations of General Warren more than two hours. . . .[6]

More problems were in store for the Federal commander that day. Just as French fell one pontoon short in spanning the river, Warren's engineers discovered that they were also one pontoon short, necessitating the construction of a trestle.

To further add to the Union army's delay at the river, French discovered that the steep southern bank of Jacob's Ford made it practically impossible to cross the artillery and wagons of the III and VI Corps. Upon learning of this additional frustrating development, Meade ordered the horse-drawn vehicles rerouted to Germanna Ford.[7]

The II, III, and V Corps finally completed crossing the Rapidan in the late afternoon of the 26th, but darkness set in before the columns of the I and VI Corps were able to reach the southern bank. Having no desire to venture into the Wilderness — the local name for the expansive area of dense woodland below the Rapidan — in the dark, Meade suspended his advance far short of his objectives for the day. The vanguard of the three Federal columns had only progressed one or two miles from the river before bivouacking for the night.

The area through which the Union troops now advanced was a potential haven for enemy bushwhackers, and required a high degree of vigilance on the part of Federal officers. Colonel Lyman described the area in a letter to his wife:

> Do you know the scrub oak woods above Hammond's Pond, a sort of growth that is hard for even a single man to force his way through for any great distance? That is the growth of most of this country, . . . and plus a great many "runs" and clay holes, where, in bad weather, vehicles sink to their axles. Along this region there are only two or three roads that can be counted on. These are the turnpike, the plank road south of it, and the plank road that runs from Germanna Ford. There are many narrow roads, winding and little known, that in good weather may serve for the slow passage of columns (though they are mere farmers' or woodcutters' thoroughfares); but a day's rain will render them impassable for waggons and artillery.[8]

The progress of his army on the 26th turned out to be a great disappointment for Meade. Having learned the day before of Major General Ulysses S. Grant's victory at Chattanooga, Tennessee, on the 24th and 25th of November, Meade might have hoped to achieve his own measure of success in Virginia.[9] That hope, however, was now in the process of being dashed on the banks of the Rapidan. As on November 24, the lack of "prompt, vigorous action" jeopardized the success of the entire campaign.[10]

Meade realized that if he was to bring the enemy to battle on Federal terms, his army would have to make much headway the next day. On the evening of the 26th, therefore, he informed his corps commanders that their troops were to unite in the vicinity of Robinson's Tavern the next morning and were to then advance about six miles to Old Verdiersville.[11] The Federals wound then be well behind the Confederate line, giving Meade the option either to cut the enemy's force in half or to sit and wait for Lee to make a desperate attack.

Meade still hoped to spring his trap on his Confederate adversary. Unfortunately for the Federal commander, however, Lee was not about to remain idle while the Yankees maneuvered behind him.

Heavy fog shrouded the Rapidan River Valley on the morning of November 26, severely restricting the view of gray-clad observers at various signal stations along the Confederate line.[12] As the fog gradually lifted, the scene revealed below seized the attention of the signal corps members. Through the thinning veil of mist they saw long columns of Yankee soldiers marching toward the lower fords of the Rapidan.

Having anticipated an enemy advance for over two weeks, word of the Union movement did not come as a complete surprise to the Confederate commander. The wait now over, Lee immediately began preparing to meet this latest Federal thrust.

As thorough as his scouting reports had been, however, Lee was still unsure of Meade's intentions once the Yankees were south of the Rapidan. In his official report of the campaign, Lee recalled his initial dilemma:

> The country in that vicinity was unfavorable for observation, being almost an unbroken forest, and it could not be discovered whether it was the design of the Federal commander to advance toward Richmond or move up the Rapidan upon our right flank.[13]

·Lee was not willing to wait, however, until Meade divulged his plan. To counter either contingency, the Confederate commander decided to attack the exposed Union flank if Meade's intent was a strike toward Richmond or to defend against a Union attack if Meade's objective was to gain the rear of the Confederate line.

Early's Second Corps was directed to advance along the Orange Turnpike and Raccoon Ford Road while Hill's Third Corps was to follow on the Orange Plank Road. Major General Wade Hampton's cavalry division was to precede Hill's troops.[14]

On the evening of November 26, for the third time in less than a month and a half, Confederate officers ordered their men to draw three days' rations and prepare to march. Roused from their comfortable camps on this frigid November evening, so cold that icicles formed on men's beards, Lee's soldiers once again prepared to confront the Federal army.[15]

While his men did not relish the thought of leaving their shelters for points unknown, Lee's spirits soared with the prospect of battle. After the setbacks at Rappahannock Station and Kelly's Ford, he finally had his chance to seize the initiative.

Warren's II Corps broke camp at daybreak on the 27th and slowly worked its way south through the Wilderness to the Orange Turnpike, where it turned west in the direction of Robinson's Tavern. Brigadier General Alexander Hays' division was in the van with Colonel Samuel S. Carroll's brigade leading the way.

At the same time Confederate General Early's division, led by remnants of Harry Hays' Louisiana Tigers (those who survived the debacle at Rappahannock Station), headed east along the Turnpike with orders to occupy the high ground adjacent to the tavern. As the opposing forces marched toward each other, they threw out skirmish lines which clashed about 100 yards west of the tavern. The time was 11:00 a.m.[16]

Unsure of the strength of the force opposing him, Confederate General Hays sent a strong skirmish line forward to feel the enemy position while he awaited the arrival of Major General Robert E. Rodes' Division. Hays described the action in his official report:

> Hoke's and Hays' brigades, under command of Col. William Monaghan [commander of the 6th Louisiana and one of the few officers to escape across the Rappahannock during the action of November 7]... were placed in position with their left resting on the pike, and Gordon's was posted on the extension of this line with his right touching Colonel Monaghan's left. Skirmishers were promptly thrown to the front and within a short distance of the enemy's main body. There being no favorable position for my artillery, and the enemy holding a line of great strength, I deemed it inexpedient to attack without co-operation, and accordingly sent a staff officer to communicate with Major-General Rodes, who, I had been informed, would be about a mile to my left.[17]

Upon his arrival, Rodes surveyed that portion of the enemy position not masked by the dense forest and decided that an attack should be postponed until Major General Edward Johnson's Division, then marching toward the pike along the Raccoon Ford Road, reached the Confederate position.[18]

Meanwhile, as the Confederate generals evaluated the situation in their front, the Federal II Corps commander, Warren, was busy deploying his men along the high ground west of the tavern. As Warren was engaged in this task, Meade, who had been following behind the II Corps, arrived on the field and advised Warren to delay any further fighting until he was reinforced by the rest of the army.[19]

Except for constant skirmish fire along the line, the opposing forces just sat and waited on the Turnpike for reinforcements to arrive. It would be another long, frustrating delay for Meade, who must have perceived himself as a spectator of lost opportunities. Unfortunately for him, however, further frustrations and disappointments would come before the conclusion of this ill-fated campaign.

While the opposing infantry skirmished along the Turnpike, Union and Confederate cavalry columns unknowingly headed toward each other on the Orange Plank Road, about three miles south of Robinson's Tavern. The Confederate force, led by its flamboyant commander, Major General J.E.B. Stuart, collided at about 11:00 a.m. with David Gregg's Federal cavalry division near New Hope Church. The terrain being densely wooded, both sides, supported by artillery, fought holding actions on foot while awaiting the arrival of infantry.[20]

Confederate General A. P. Hill's men rushed down the Plank Road to relieve Stuart's troops, Brigadier General Henry H. Walker's Brigade of Major General Henry Heth's Division in the lead.[21] At about 2:30 p.m., Walker's skirmishers reached the front. His infantrymen, however, were held in check by Gregg's troopers until these Yankees were relieved at about 3:00 p.m. by the vanguard of Sykes' V Corps.

It had taken the V Corps six hours to advance from Parker's Store to New Hope Church, a distance of only three miles. Due to this delay, "Tardy George," as Sykes had been called in the regular army because of habitual lateness,[22] missed an opportunity to gain the high ground west of New Hope Church; once his corps arrived, this choice terrain was already in the hands of Hill's troops.

Upon establishing communications with army headquarters, Sykes was ordered by Meade to halt his advance and hold his position until the III Corps reached Warren's flank. It was after 4:00 p.m. and the Federals were still not in the position Meade had hoped to achieve more than 24 hours earlier.

One fact that the Union commander could have found solace in, had he known, was that Lee was still unaware of the Federals' intent. The Confederate general had been following Hill's corps down the Plank Road and was present when Heth's division engaged the enemy. He still had been unable to determine if the Federal forces along the Turnpike and Plank Road were only diversions while the main body of the Army of the Potomac raced for the Richmond, Fredericksburg, and Potomac Railroad, or if they were the advance elements of the enemy army, intent on giving battle to his vastly outnumbered force.[23]

Lee was unwilling to commit his troops to a general engagement without definite intelligence of the enemy's movements, information which was difficult to gather due to the densely wooded nature of the Wilderness. In addition, Edward Johnson's division of Early's corps had not yet arrived in position north of the pike.

The Confederate commander, therefore, postponed an attack until adequate intelligence was gathered and he was at full force. If he feared his army was in immediate jeopardy it was an idle concern, since Meade was also reluctant to bring on a general engagement without his full command on the field.

As the day progressed and the Federal I, III, and VI Corps had not yet reached the field, Meade became concerned about the security of the II and V Corps, deployed three miles apart. Just as the dense forest made it impossible for Lee to determine the Federals' intent, it also masked the disposition of Confederate forces along the Union front. For all Meade knew, the whole Army of Northern Virginia could have been massing to attack his two isolated corps at any moment. Since the I Corps followed closely behind the V, he was less concerned about the safety of Sykes' troops than he was about Warren's.[24] It was almost noon and Meade had yet to hear from either French or Sedgwick, who were somewhere in the Wilderness north of the Turnpike.

Since Prince's division of French's III Corps had bivouacked less than five miles from Robinson's Tavern the previous evening, Meade found it difficult to understand why, by 11:00 a.m., he had not yet heard from French. At 11:00 a.m. and again at 11:15 a.m. Meade sent dispatches to French notifying him of the presence of the enemy in Warren's front, just west of the tavern, necessitating the swift arrival of the III and VI Corps. Because of the difficult terrain, Meade's messengers to French found it necessary to travel by way of the Germanna Road, a circuitous distance of more than twelve miles. Meade would not have felt any more at ease had he known how things were progressing on his right.[25]

After the delays of the 26th, which French placed squarely on Prince's shoulders, the corps commander may have desired to change the vanguard of his column. Maneuverability within the Wilderness, however, was practically non-existent. Prince's division, therefore, continued to lead the corps.

The division had started its march without incident at daybreak, but only progressed a little more than a mile from Jacob's Ford before it halted at a fork in the road adjacent to the Widow Morris' Farm. Prince learned from his rough map of the roads through this dense forest that the branch to the right was the most direct to Robinson's Tavern, but it led him in the direction of the enemy position at Bartlett's Mill and merged with the Raccoon Ford Road, which he could assume was at the very least picketed by Confederate troops. The road to his left, however, was the more circuitous route and would delay his union with Warren.

Unsure of the best course of action, Prince sent a cavalry detachment down the left fork to establish communication with Warren and sent another mounted unit to the right to reconnoiter for enemy troops. The latter force soon returned with information that Confederate cavalry blocked the road.[26]

While Prince's troops were stalled on the road between the Widow Morris' Farm and Jacob's Ford, French and his staff pushed their way through the clogged, narrow passage, bordered by a dense forest, to discover the source of the holdup and to establish headquarters in a farm dwelling close to the front. By this time considerable friction existed between Prince and the corps commander. French reasoned that the delays of the day before and this present holdup were primarily due to Prince's habitual slowness.[27]

The III Corps commander, however, seemed to be functioning under his own deficiencies and became the butt of many jokes by his troops. French had a longstanding reputation as a "drunkard." It was later charged that he remained in the farmhouse, drunk, throughout the day. In numerous accounts of the events of the 27th, it has been reported that French obviously appeared as if he had been heavily drinking and was openly subjected to catcalls like "old Blinky" and "old gin barrel." The charges of drunkenness would later be used to explain his inability to take charge on the 27th, his vacillation in issuing orders, and his complete disregard for or misunderstanding of Meade's orders.[28]

The ultimate cause of the problem, however, was not the real issue. The fact that Prince and French were not working well together caused serious problems for Meade and would be cited as one of the reasons for the campaign's failure.[29]

After establishing his headquarters in the farmhouse, French sent an aide forward to learn the source of this delay at the Widow Morris', a task he might easily have done himself, being only about 300 yards from Prince's position.

It wasn't until about 10:00 a.m. that the scouts, having established contact with Warren, reported back to Prince.[30] The division commander immediately informed French that while the route to the right was heavily picketed by enemy cavalry, the one to the left, although longer, was open. Prince waited for French's reply.[31] The delay might be singled out as one of the significant turning points of the campaign; for had Prince immediately taken either route, he could have linked with Warren's right flank within a few hours. Meade's line could have then pushed forward against little opposition to seize the high ground to the west.

While Prince's division was stalled at the crossroads, Meade finally received his first communication from French at about 11:30 a.m. Its text must have added to Meade's concern over the competence of his III Corps commander: "The head of my column is near the plank road [turnpike], and waiting for General Warren."[32] Actually, French's column was more than three miles from the Turnpike at the time.

Meade's impatience, having grown to the point of rage, was evident in his reply, through Humphreys, to French:

> Your dispatch of 9.20 is received. What are you waiting for? No orders have been sent you to wait for General Warren anywhere upon your route. Robertson's Tavern is the point where he takes precedence and he is there now engaged with the enemy who are in strong force. He is waiting for you. The commanding general directs that you move forward as rapidly as possible to Robertson's Tavern, where your corps is wanted.[33]

Prior to receiving this dispatch from Meade, French, still in the farm house, had sent Prince a dispatch ordering him to take the road to the right and demanding to know what the division commander intended to do.

Relieved of the responsibility for choosing the route of march, Prince replied by dispatch, "I shall first take the road (in military parlance), and having obtained possession of it, I shall reconnoiter and act according to circumstances."[34] He deployed the brigade of Colonel William Blaisdell along the fringe of a clearing a short distance down the road from Widow Morris'. The 1st Massachusetts Infantry was sent forward as skirmishers and the guns of Lieutenant John Bucklyn's Battery E, 1st Rhode Island Light Artillery, which had done a commendable job at Kelly's Ford almost three weeks earlier, were placed in the clearing. Prince ordered the 1st Massachusetts to feel out the enemy position before sending the rest of his division forward.[35]

Meade, meanwhile, was perplexed by a later dispatch from French reporting the presence of enemy troops in Prince's front. Were these enemy troops reinforcing the Confederates already on the Turnpike, or was Lee attempting to turn the Federal right flank? Whatever his opponent's intentions, Meade realized more than ever the importance of uniting his army. The Federal commander therefore ordered French to attack the enemy in his front while at the same time "throwing your left forward so as to connect with General Warren at Robertson's Tavern." He emphasized that the sole purpose of this attack was to join Warren.[36]

It was now 2:00 p.m. and Prince had been stalled for more than five hours. As Union General Marsena Patrick later recounted in his diary: "Of course there was a good deal of surprise & dissatisfaction felt by all, at this want of cooperation on the part of French but Meade became very greatly out of temper about it. . . ."[37]

For the second straight day, Meade helplessly watched his plan fall far short of its goal due to delays and inept leadership on his right flank. Luckily for Lee, chance placed the troops of one of his more aggressive division commanders opposite the stalled Federal III Corps.

Major General Edward Johnson, commanding a division of Ewell's Second Corps, received orders early on November 27 to proceed by way of Raccoon Ford Road to Locust Grove, just west of Robinson's Tavern, to anchor the left flank of the corps line. He immediately set his division in motion: Brigadier General John M. Jones' Brigade led the march followed by the brigades of Brigadier General Leroy A. Stafford and Brigadier General James A. Walker. A portion of Lieutenant Colonel R. Snowden Andrews' artillery battalion and ambulance wagons followed close behind Walker. Brigadier General George H. Steuart's Brigade was chosen by Johnson to bring up the rear.

Johnson ordered each brigade commander to deploy skirmishers along the left flank of the marching column since he had been informed the day before that an enemy force of unknown strength had crossed the Rapidan at Jacob's Ford. It was not Confederate cavalry but actually these skirmishers whom Prince's scouts had engaged while reconnoitering in the direction of Raccoon Ford Road. After quickly driving the blue coats away, Johnson's men continued their march.

Throughout the morning of the 27th, little more than a mile south of Widow Morris', where Prince's division was stalled, Johnson's troops advanced toward the Orange Turnpike. It was around noon when Jones' brigade reached Rodes' left flank. Regimental commanders were in the act of deploying skirmishers in their front when Johnson, who had been accompanying Jones, received disturbing news from Steuart. The ambulance train had been attacked by enemy skirmishers whom Steuart assumed were dismounted cavalry.[38]

The 47-year-old division commander had been well schooled in military tactics. A graduate of West Point, Johnson had served in both the Seminole and Mexican Wars, being twice brevetted for gallant and meritorious service in the latter campaign. A native Virginian, he resigned from the regular army in 1861 to join the Confederate cause. Excluding a year of recuperation due to a severe ankle wound received during "Stonewall" Jackson's 1862 Valley Campaign, he had served with distinction on several battlefields with the Army of Northern Virginia.[39]

Experience had long ago taught Johnson never to assume anything when encountering the enemy. Realizing there was no substitute for personal observation, Johnson hurried to the rear to judge the situation for himself. By the time he arrived, Steuart's brigade had already become heavily engaged with Federal infantry.

Reacting swiftly to this unexpected enemy thrust, Johnson recalled his other three brigades and deployed them along the road facing the Payne farmsteads. The terrain was part of the Wilderness with small patches of open farmland surrounded by thick forests.

Jones' brigade anchored Johnson's right flank, Stafford's brigade the right center, with Walker's on the left center and Steuart's on the far left.[40] Guns from Snowden Andrew's artillery battalion were placed along the line. The limited field of vision, due to the density of the woods, not only made deploying troops difficult but also restricted a commander's control over the units engaged, and, except for small patches of clearing, neutralized the effect of artillery.

Johnson ordered his brigade commanders to throw skirmishers forward to determine the length and strength of the enemy line. His officers struggled to maintain order and to keep their men oriented in the right direction to avoid accidently firing into friendly units. Still, they found it nearly impossible to determine the strength and extent of the Federals' line. One Confederate veteran recalled:

> They [Johnson's skirmishers] are confronted either by a line of skirmishers vastly outnumbering them, or by a close line of troops; they are checked and have to be re-inforced to enable them to hold their ground . . . . It seemed as if the enemy was throwing minie-balls upon us by the bucket-full, when the battle got fairly under way.[41]

While the nature of the terrain created a great deal of confusion along the battle line, a like amount of confusion reigned at Union III Corps headquarters.

Having received French's order to advance to the right, Prince had just begun to deploy his troops when he was stunned by an order from French to cease his advance. The corps commander had determined that the road to the right was the wrong route. This was only the first of two delays instigated by French which not only led to greater confusion in the Federal ranks but also gave Johnson's troops ample time to form along the Raccoon Ford Road.[42]

Following the receipt of the first order to cease his advance, Prince personally reported to corps headquarters and confronted French. Once he advised the corps commander of the situation at the front, he was ordered to continue the advance, and was directed by French to call on Brigadier General Joseph B. Carr's division for support if necessary.

Discovering that the enemy line was longer than his own, Prince rode to Carr's headquarters and requested his support. Carr, however, declined to give it. Prince recounted the meeting in his report:

> I replied, "But I order it." [Carr] begged me to understand that it was with no personal view toward me that he declined, but that his instructions were to follow. I immediately communicated this in writing to the major-general commanding the corps, and received for answer by the person who bore it, "The general says go on."[43]

Prince had already begun to advance when, for the second time, French ordered him to halt, this time to wait for Carr to deploy on his left.

It was now about 4:00 p.m., almost four hours since Prince's force had made initial contact with the enemy. Now he waited while Carr's division struggled through the Wilderness to a position bordering the Payne farmstead. French had directed Carr to communicate, if possible, with the right flank of the II Corps.[44] This was an impossible request since Warren's command was more than two miles away. French not only seemed to be out of touch with his own corps' situation, as evidenced by the vacillating orders to Prince, but he also did not seem to know where he was in relation to the Turnpike and the rest of the army.

As Carr's men arrived at their position, Johnson had completed his reconnaissance of the Federal line. Discovering that it was no longer than his own, Johnson decided to seize the initiative. He ordered forward his division, totaling 5,300 men, still unaware that he faced the Union III Corps with the VI in close support — more than 32,000 enemy troops.[45] Although Johnson was overwhelmingly outnumbered, the fact that the field of battle was primarily wilderness significantly worked to his advantage.

Finding his right flank free of enemy troops, Johnson ordered Jones' and Stafford's brigades to wheel to the left — a difficult maneuver when performed on the parade ground, let alone in dense growth where visual contact was virtually impossible. As a result, the four Confederate brigades attacked the enemy piecemeal. As Jones' men wheeled into position, they discovered the rest of the division deployed behind a fence about 200 yards from the Federal line.[46]

The combined thrust of Jones' and Stafford's brigades drove Carr's division back, completely routing the Federal left flank. Major General David B. Birney rushed his division forward to reinforce Carr and quickly stabilized the Federal position.

With night rapidly approaching, the momentum of battle swung back and forth as troops on both sides charged and counter-charged across the broken, wooded countryside. At one point Captain John C. Johnson, a rather rotund officer of the 50th Virginia Infantry of Jones' brigade, became so enraged when his men cowered behind a ridge to escape enemy projectiles that he stretched himself out along the crest and offered his body as a breastwork to anyone afraid to advance. One Confederate later recalled the incident:

> Several of [Johnson's men] very promptly accepted his challenge, lying down behind him, resting their guns on him, firing steadily from this position until the fight was over. I am happy to say that the gallant captain was not injured.[47]

Leadership by exemplary behavior was not limited to company or even regimental officers. Each of the brigade commanders personally took charge of deploying his men in the confusion of the Wilderness. Both Steuart and Jones were wounded while at the head of their commands.

When one of his regiments faltered under an intense fire, General Walker "seized the colors," General Johnson stated in his report, "leaped his horse over a fence into an open field in front of his command, and waved his men on, while the lines of the enemy, 80 yards distant, directed a fearful converging fire upon him. General Stafford acted with similar daring, but, fortunately, neither was wounded."[48]

Many officers and men looked on in amazement as Stafford conspicuously rode back and forth along his brigade's firing line, as if in a frenzy, stopping only long enough to send troops to critical points in his line. While Stafford never was one to worry about personal safety in the heat of conflict, his real reason for racing recklessly along the front was that his horse, "Harry Hays," was excited by the fire and activity, requiring constant movement.

When Stafford rode back to redirect artillery fire he was confronted by an artillery officer who asked, "General who was that crazy fellow on horse-back trying to get himself killed and at the same time show off by prancing his horse up and down the line of fire?"

"Oh!" replied Stafford, stifling a grin, "that was one of the officers in my brigade." With that, he raced back to the front.[49]

Johnson also advanced to the division front, directing troop movements. He used a massive club as a walking stick due to his shattering ankle wound more than a year earlier. When his horse was shot from under him during the Battle of Payne's Farm, Johnson was seen brandishing the club to encourage his men. The intense fire became too much for even "Old Clubby" (one of several nicknames Johnson's colorful character so easily evoked), however, and one of Steuart's aides, First

Lieutenant McHenry Howard, saw Johnson "hunching his shoulders and not disdaining the partial shelter to his broad person of a small tree — there were no large trees about there. While I stopped and talked with him the bullets coming through the switchy woods sounded somewhat like the hissing of a hail or sleet storm."[50]

This fight might have been limited in scope, only involving one Confederate and less than three Federal divisions, but it was fierce nonetheless. McHenry Howard recalled:

> We did not mind the artillery fire but the musket balls flew very thick.... Altogether, it was an interesting and in some respects a picturesque battle — the unexpected suddenness of its opening, the changes of position and encounters in the woods which covered the ground, and other features."[51]

Officers on both sides called for more ammunition and reinforcements during the intense action, but darkness brought an end to the fight before the front line troops were relieved. Johnson's men fell back to the Raccoon Ford Road while their Federal counterparts withdrew to the woods, ending what had been a relatively contained but costly engagement for each side. Johnson's division sustained 545 casualties during the fight at Payne's Farm while the Union III Corps lost 952 men.[52]

The most significant aspect of the battle was not which side won or lost, but the fact that Johnson's division, although outnumbered almost six to one, halted the advance of both the Federal III and VI Corps. In his memoirs, General Early recognized the contribution of Johnson's men on this day:

> ... by the check thus given to the enemy in this quarter saved the whole corps from a very serious disaster, for if the enemy had got possession of this road [Raccoon Ford], he would have been able to come up in rear of the other division, while they were confronting the large force at Locust Grove.[53]

By checking the advance of the Federal III and VI Corps, the latter remaining bottled up near Jacob's Ford throughout most of the day, Johnson ultimately neutralized the whole Army of the Potomac. Lee's entire force was in a secure position by nightfall, dashing Meade's hopes to dictate the terms of the campaign.

Throughout November 27, Meade and his staff had helplessly monitored the actions along the army's front. Instead of the Federals quickly converging near the tavern and attacking the enemy before he could concentrate, the day was wasted by uncoordinated, insignificant actions along three separate fronts.

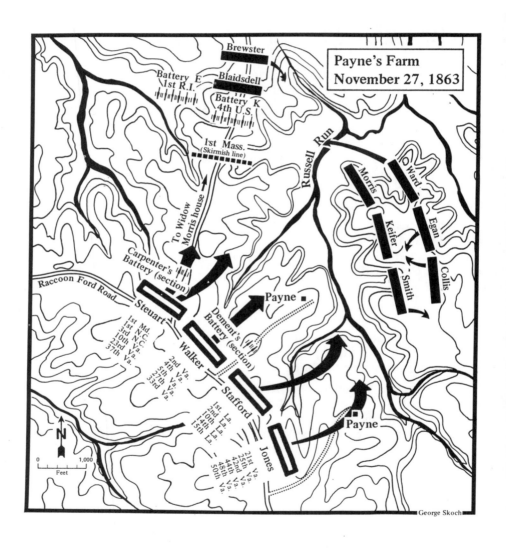

Payne's Farm
November 27, 1863

Brewster

Battery E
1st R.I.

Blaidsdell

Battery K
4th U.S.

1st Mass.
(Skirmish line)

Russell Run

Ward

Morris

Keifer

Egan

Collis

Smith

To Widow Morris house

Carpenter's
Battery (section)

Raccoon Ford Road

Steuart

Payne

1st Md.
1st N.C.
3rd Va.
10th Va.
23rd Va.
37th Va.

Dement's
Battery (section)

Walker

2nd Va.
4th Va.
5th Va.
27th Va.
33rd Va.

Stafford

1st La.
2nd La.
10th La.
14th La.
15th La.

Jones

21st Va.
25th Va.
42nd Va.
44th Va.
48th Va.
50th Va.

Payne

N

0   1,000
Feet

George Skoch

Frustrated by the delays, particularly on his right flank, Meade realized that his plan for "stealing a march" on Lee had failed miserably. Hoping to regain the initiative, which had now slipped from his hands, Meade planned to launch an attack on the Confederate position the next morning.

Throughout the night Meade concentrated his army along a line perpendicular to the Turnpike just west of Robinson's Tavern with the I Corps on the left flank, the II in the center, and the VI on the right. These three commands were to attack the Confederate center at daybreak. The III and V Corps would remain in reserve.[54]

While Meade prepared his army for the morning attack, Lee evaluated his intelligence reports. Neither commander had firmly controlled the events of November 27. Essentially, they both had remained close to their headquarters throughout the day, assessed reports that came in from their subordinates, and issued whatever orders they could to maintain some semblance of control over their commands.

The two most significant pieces of intelligence received by Lee were the report of the strength of the troops confronting Johnson on the Confederate left flank, and a dispatch from Brigadier General Thomas L. Rosser that his cavalry brigade had attacked and routed the ordnance train of the I and V Corps. More important than the fact that the train was put to flight was that it was heading west toward Orange Court House. Lee was now convinced that his army, and not Richmond, was Meade's ultimate objective.[55]

Determining that his present position was not favorable for defense, Lee ordered his entire line to fall back during the night of the 27th to the higher terrain west of Mine Run. The Confederates diligently worked throughout the cold damp night constructing formidable works in anticipation of a Federal attack. Captain Robert E. Park of the 12th Alabama Infantry later recalled the activity on the frantic afternoon and evening of the 27th.

> While skirmishing, the brigade in the rear was busily employed throwing up breastworks of poles and earth, latter dug up with picks made of sharpened oak poles and bayonets, and thrown on the logs and brush with tin plates and cups, and bare hands. It is marvelous with what rapidity a fortification sufficiently strong to resist minie balls can be thrown up. A sense of danger quickens a man's energies.[56]

So far these men had benefited from good luck in addition to an extreme degree of inept leadership on the part of the Union command. They realized, however, that it was just a matter of time before they would once again meet their opponents in battle. Many were convinced that the morning would bring the anticipated conflict. Lee's men, therefore, grimly labored through the bleak cold night preparing for whatever developments dawn would bring.

Gouverneur K. Warren, Major General, U.S.A.

Harry Thompson Hays, Brigadier General, C.S.A.

George Hume Steuart, Brigadier General, C.S.A.

Edward Johnson, Major General, C.S.A.

William French, Major General, U.S.A.

Henry Prince, Brigadier General, U.S.A.

John Sedgwick, Major General, U.S.A.

David Russell, Brigadier General, U.S.A.

This modern view (looking west) along Virginia State Route 20 – the old Orange Turnpike — closely resembles the terrain depicted in the illustration below. The camera position is on a rise approximately one mile west of Locust Grove.

Opposing lines at Mine Run.

A modern view of the 'Widow Morris crossroad' (looking southwest), located at the intersection of Virginia State Route 603 and a dead end road (on the left.) After much confusion and delay Prince's division approached the Payne Farm battlefield on the road to the right.

Author's photograph

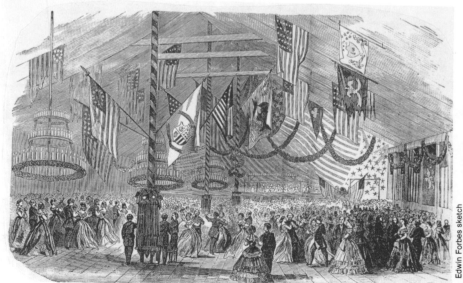

Edwin Forbes sketch

Washington's Birthday celebration staged by the 2nd Corps.

Action at Morton's Ford, Virginia, evening, February 6, 1864.

The William Britton House. Located on a bluff west of Mine Run, behind earthworks on the Confederate left flank, the house served as a hospital during the Mine Run Campaign. This sketch, by descendant Mr. Warren Ernst, is based on the recollections of family members. The house no longer stands.

65

Fight at Kelly's Ford, November 7, 1863, viewed from behind Captain Henry Jacob Sleeper's 10th Massachusetts Battery.

Courtesy: Library of Congress. Detail from a sketch by Alfred A. Waud

Site of pontoon bridge

Confederate battery positions

This modern composite photograph of the Rappahannock Station battlefield shows the ground much as it appears in the illustration below. The view is looking north from near the area occupied by the 54th and 6th North Carolina infantry regiments.

Detail from a sketch by Edwin Forbes

Sedgwick's assault (looking north) over the ground depicted in the photograph above.

This sketch of Meade's troops recrossing to the north bank of the Rappahannock River at Rappahannock Station (October, 1863) shows the pontoon bridge and the fortifications on the south bank — occupied by Dance's Battery during the November 7, engagement.

Detail from a sketch by Edwin Forbes.

Sedgwick's assault (looking west) viewed from east of the Orange and Alexandria Railroad track. The 5th Corps skirmish line is shown in the foreground.

Detail from a sketch by Edwin Forbes.

CHAPTER IV

"I Cannot Be Party to a Wanton Slaughter"

General Meade rode in advance of his command on the morning of November 28 to study personally the enemy's line west of Mine Run. The fact that the Confederates had fallen back to this position during the night had come as a surprise to the Federal commander.

At dawn the I, II, and VI Corps advanced expecting to find the enemy in their immediate front. What they found instead were abandoned works and a trail of discarded debris leading in the direction of Mine Run.

When Meade discovered that the Confederates had abandoned their line, he ordered the pursuit to continue west, Warren's II Corps in the lead. Heavy rains hampered the advance.

Once Meade developed the enemy position, he faced the slow, painstaking process of deploying in the Wilderness. Union Colonel Lyman relayed the following account of the frustrating delays of the morning in a letter to his wife:

> This was a tremendous job, in the narrow wood-roads, deep with mud; and occupied fully the whole day. If you consider that the men must often move by fours, then a division of 4000 men, closed up, would occupy in marching some 1000 yards, and, by adding the space for pack horses, and the usual gaps and intervals, it would be nearer a mile; so you see how an army would string out, even with no artillery. You must remember also that these long columns cannot move over two miles in an hour; often not so much. . . .[1]

Having struggled into position, the scene across Mine Run which greeted Meade and his troops was enough to tempt even the most steadfast commander to call off this whole affair. Meade found the western bank of Mine Run "crowned with infantry parapets, abatis, and epaulements for batteries." To reach the enemy line the Federals would have to cross the run, "in many places swampy and impassable," and charge about 1,000 yards up a cleared, gradual slope well covered by enemy artillery.[2]

A member of the Federal II Corps later sent a local paper his own account of the situation along Mine Run on the morning of November 28:

> I never saw a more imposing sight — the red battle-flags, with the large white cross in the centre, flying — a long, dark col-

69

umn of men, their bright arms gleaming in the morning sun — the dark and frowning muzzles of eighteen or twenty pieces of artillery, and all as quiet and still as though not a soul but the once peaceful and happy inhabitants of the valley were near.[3]

To the relief of the frontline troops, who were anticipating an order to attack, Meade spent the remainder of the 28th studying the enemy's position and weighing alternatives.

That evening General Warren proposed a movement on the enemy right flank for the purpose of either finding a vulnerable spot for attack or turning the flank, by maneuvering to the enemy rear, thereby forcing Lee to abandon his line.[4] Meade trusted the judgement of his II Corps commander, the hero of Gettysburg. Warren had great self confidence (some called it arrogance)[5] and had demonstrated good tactical judgement not only at Gettysburg, where he saved the Federal left flank along Cemetery Ridge by securing Little Round Top, but also at Bristoe Station, where his riflemen dealt a shattering defeat to A. P. Hill's corps.

After brief contemplation, since few alternatives actually existed, Meade approved Warren's plan. Under the II Corps commander's direction, his force, with the addition of one division of the VI Corps, three artillery batteries, and 300 cavalrymen — a total of about 18,000 men — were to maneuver around the enemy's right flank.[6] Meade instructed the other corps commanders to examine the enemy's position in their fronts to determine whether an assault could be successful.

It was unfortunate for the Federal commander that the necessity of a flanking movement had not presented itself the previous day, for at that time he had the V and I Corps well situated on the Plank Road, ready to turn the Confederate right flank. Now the II Corps and its supports would practically have to retrace the steps of the V Corps, a march of more then eleven miles over the rough, wilderness roads, complicated even more by frequent storms.

Meade found himself in the spot which he had so desperately sought to avoid. Lee was in a position to dictate the terms of an engagement over ground of the Confederate commander's choosing. Meade had fallen into the same trap which had caught some of the army's previous commanders. He had fallen victim to the tactical skills of his opponent.

With Lee well prepared for his next move, Meade's only hope was to discover and take advantage of whatever opportunities, if any, Lee opened to him. Meade realized that he must not be impulsive while, at the same time, he must be aggressive — a difficult task in the face of such a formidable opponent. By now, even with the string of successes at Gettysburg, Bristoe Station, Rappahannock Station, and Kelly's Ford to his credit, the responsibilities of command must have weighed heavily on

Meade's shoulders. The memories of his two predecessors, Hooker and Burnside, shaking in their boots at the end of their bouts with Lee must have stood paramount in Meade's mind.

Throughout the 28th the Confederates strengthened their position, skirmished with the enemy, and awaited a Federal attack. Early deployed Hays' division astride the turnpike, with Rodes' division to its left and Johnson's anchoring the left flank of the Confederate line.

. On Early's immediate right, Hill placed Major General Richard H. Anderson's Division, with Major General Cadmus M. Wilcox's Division in the center of Hill's line, crossing the Plank Road, and Heth's division holding down Hill's right flank, supported by Wade Hampton's cavalry.[7]

Lee was satisfied with the strength and security of his line, making only minor adjustments throughout the day. His infantrymen worked tirelessly on their entrenchments west of Mine Run, constructing an almost impregnable line, as they watched Meade deploy his army along a ridge only a few hundred yards to the east.

In an effort to determine the Yankees' next move, Lee sent Hampton's division, on the evening of the 28th, under J.E.B. Stuart's personal command, down the Plank Road, which had been virtually abandoned by Federal troops, in an attempt to gain the enemy's rear and "ascertain his purpose."

Stuart's troopers met and easily drove back a brigade of Union cavalry at Parker's Store, capturing equipment and more than 100 prisoners. Confederate reinforcements enabled Stuart to press the enemy back toward the Rapidan. Before a complete Federal rout developed, however, Stuart learned that a column of Union infantry had marched south from the Turnpike and was advancing west along the Plank Road, threatening the Confederate right flank. With captured prisoners and supplies in hand, Stuart rushed back to the main line to strengthen the flank and to inform Lee about the Yankee advance.[8]

Those troops threatening the Confederate right flank were the men of Warren's command, who began their march a short time before dawn on the 29th. The II Corps commander described the march in his official report:

No inconsiderable preparations were required to issue rations, dispose of surplus trains, relieve our line, etc., along the enemy's front, and all combined determined me not to start till daybreak. The night was dark and stormy, and our route, after going to the rear as far as Robertson's Tavern, lay through woods along bad roads. . . . Our march on the 29th was rapid and unobstructed, until we reached (about 10.30 [a.m.]) the cavalry outposts of General Gregg on the plank road. Our march up to this point was 8 miles.[9]

It was in the vicinity of New Hope Church that Warren's column encountered enemy vedettes, behind whom there seemed to be extensive entrenchments which later turned out to be the bank of an unfinished railroad. Not taking any chances, Warren formed a line of attack and at 1:00 p.m. began to push the enemy pickets back toward the main Confederate position. Throughout this movement, Warren attempted to mask the strength of his force from Confederate observation since he hoped to deceive Lee as to the Federals' true intent.

Once his command reached Mine Run, Warren began to deploy his troops around the enemy right flank. His men met with some resistance but were able to push forward to the base of the ridge crowned by a light line of enemy works. His true intent unmasked by the deployment of his command around the Confederate flank, Warren prepared for an assault.

Before Warren could launch the assault, however, he received disturbing news from General Gregg. The Federal cavalry had been attacked by Stuart's force at Parker's Store, only a few miles in Warren's rear. Believing that Lee might be attempting his own turning movement around the Union left flank, the II Corps commander suspended his advance while he attempted to determine what was taking place behind him. He soon discovered, however, that it was only a detachment of Confederate cavalry which had already returned to the enemy line. Now Warren could again turn his full attention to the Confederate position in his front.

"We had passed Mine Run," Warren wrote in his report, "it was no longer an obstacle, and there was no stream nor commanding ground between us and their base of supplies. . . ."[10] He felt that he was on the verge of a great victory. One coordinated push, he reasoned, and the Confederate line would collapse. There was a problem, however, over which Warren had no control.

As Lieutenant Colonel Francis A. Walker, the II Corps assistant adjutant-general, later recalled, the enemy works were "slight and thinly occupied. . . . success seemed to be within our grasp, and so it would have been but for one circumstance — the day was nearly spent."[11] Warren decided "there was not time to advance farther."[12] Although it was not much later than 5:00 p.m., the winter daylight ran out on the Federal effort.

As a result, Warren suspended any further advance that day. Realizing that his movement had been discovered by the enemy, he "made all the fires I could, my object being to make a demonstration of heavy force."[13] He then personally reported to army headquarters to inform Meade of his situation.

Earlier in the day Meade had decided to attack the enemy line on both flanks and the center, but Warren's personal report on the evening of the 29th caused him to alter that plan.

At 8 p.m. General Warren reported in person . . . expressing such confidence in his ability to carry everything before him as to induce him to give the opinion that he did not believe the enemy would remain over night, so completely did he command him. The earnest confidence that General Warren expressed of his ability to carry everything before him, and the reliance I placed on that officer's judgement. . . induced me to modify my plan. . . .[14]

General Wright, a division commander in the VI Corps, had informed Meade that the enemy's left flank, which was near the Britton Farm, although formidable was far from impregnable. The Federal commander therefore ordered the V and VI Corps, under General Sedgwick's direction, to attack that portion of the Confederate line the next morning.

The troops under Warren's command — the addition of two divisions of the III Corps giving him six divisions totaling 28,000 men — would attack the Confederate right flank.[15] The I Corps and the remaining division of the III Corps would feign an assault on the Confederate center, pushing forward if either of the attacks on the flanks should succeed.

The Federal artillery on the right was to open at 8:00 a.m. followed immediately by the attack of Warren's force. Sedgwick's troops were to advance at 9:00 a.m.[16]

Meade was confident of the success of his plan. He hoped that Warren was correct in his opinion that Lee might abandon his line by the morning. Meade must have thought, perhaps, that he had finally gained the advantage over his crafty opponent. It was a long night for the Federal commander, who anxiously awaited the morning's developments.

If Meade and Warren felt that they had finally bullied the Confederates into giving up without a fight, they had a great deal to learn about the strong resolve of Lee and his army. Warren's movement around the Confederate right attracted A. P. Hill's attention to the weaknesses of this part of his line. "If [Warren] hoped to intimidate the enemy," the Comte de Paris later wrote, "he was greatly mistaken. Hill, well warned, brings back all his forces on the south of the plank road, thus opposing about twenty thousand men to the twenty-six thousand [actually 28,000] of his adversary, and hastily constructs a few intrenchments."[17]

Throughout the night Hill's men strengthened their position with whatever tools they could find. "We had no tools except one axe to each company and made spades of plank," a Confederate infantryman wrote home. "These answered the purpose very well and it took us but a very short time to make a very good entrenchment, for every man worked hard."[18]

Due to the strength of their defenses, many Confederates looked forward to a Union attack with anticipation. One Federal officer later recalled how "Jackson's old corps had worked like beavers all night and kept themselves in a sweat 'to give the Yanks a warm reception in the morning.' They were in high glee, full of frolic and anxious to have us venture."[19]

The feelings of most of Lee's men, however, were more accurately echoed by a young Virginian in a letter to his mother: "It is very evident that both Gen. Lee & the Yankee Gen. are very cautious about bringing on a general fight & when the fight does come off, it will most probably be a desperate struggle & a drawn battle with heavy loss of life on both sides."[20]

The uncertainty as to when the assault would occur was very difficult on the Confederates deployed along the line throughout the night. One soldier remembered that they had to "keep all of our things on all the time and one-half of the men up all night, in case of an attack."[21]

While the strain of the long, cold, miserable wait took its toll on Lee's troops, the pressure was far greater on the enemy assault force deployed less than 600 yards away.

It was also a long and extremely cold night for the men of the Army of the Potomac. Fires were forbidden in the front ranks of the Federal line and many men passed the night without tents, shelters, or sleep. "Though the drooping eyelids called pitifully for sleep, each soldier knew that to sleep uncovered in that bitter air would be the sleep of death."[22] "The thermometer was below zero," another veteran remembered. "Water was frozen solid in our canteens. The bitter, chilling wind had congealed every vital current in our bodies."[23] Pickets were relieved every half hour to keep them from freezing to death.

The temperature was not the only reason for little sleep. The men under Warren's command could not help but hear a great deal of activity from the direction of the enemy line. They knew that the Confederates were spending the night strengthening the position the Federals were to attack the next morning.

The wait throughout this cold, seemingly endless night was perhaps the most difficult of the war for these Union troops. "That night," one later recalled, "there was fought in men's hearts the hardest battle of the whole war."[24] Another Yankee remembered:

It was terribly uncomfortable lying upon the frozen ground hour after hour waiting for the signal to spring to their feet and dash forward into the face of death, and the men would almost have welcomed the command, since it would have stirred the blood and warmed the benumbed limbs, but it did not come."[25]

At 3:00 a.m. the order finally did come to fall in along the Federal line. Quietly the men on the Union left flank roused themselves and advanced through the darkness to their places in the battle line.

Once formed, they were told the following by their regimental officers: the attack was to begin at 8:00 a.m.; during the charge they were not to fire until ordered; and any man going to the rear who was not wounded was to be shot. The men were also instructed to carry a blanket in which to wrap themselves in case they were wounded on the field. Otherwise, lying exposed in this temperature would mean certain death.

The order having been read, the officers instructed their men to unsling haversacks and knapsacks and stack them to the rear of each regiment. One lucky soul from each unit was chosen to guard these possessions during the assault.[26]

Having been placed at rest, some of Warren's men sat or laid on the ground, attempting to keep warm. Some, alone in their thoughts, stared blankly ahead in the darkness toward the enemy line, while others talked in hushed tones.

The dim light of daybreak slowly unveiled the Confederate position to those lucky enough, or by some accounts unlucky enough, to be stationed at the front of the battle line. As those not yet able to look at their objective confronted those who had, the common response was that a charge would result in another Fredericksburg.[27]

Chaplain H. S. Stevens of the 14th Connecticut Infantry recalled his thoughts and observations of the morning almost twenty years later:

They had, during the night, prepared strong and high works of timber and earth, with abattis, in front of us and stretching far away to our right. It was plain that they could pour upon us a heavy fire in front and an enfilading fire from a long distance .... So confident were the rebels of success that they stood in crowds upon their works and tauntingly beckoned us to come on. One cannoneer, in charge of a single light gun, pushed down upon a road passing the extreme right of their fortification, would run down two or three rods in advance of his piece, beating his hands to warm them, and making earnest signs for us to come on, and then return to his gun and wait.[28]

One member of the 15th Massachusetts remembered his thoughts as he observed the enemy line: "To a soldier who has seen two and a half years of active service engineering becomes a study, and the most of us knew that when our line should reach a certain point it would melt away like snow. There was no cover at hand for the wounded, and I for one made up my mind that I'd got to die."[29]

A deadly silence pervaded the left flank of the Union line as the foot soldiers stoically resolved to charge a position they felt was impregnable. Those with metallic identity badges on their caps removed them and pinned them to their coats or blouses. Others wrote their names, companies and regiments on slips of paper and likewise fastened them to their clothing. Mechanically they fixed their cartridge and cap boxes so that they would remain open during the charge.[30]

As 8:00 a.m. drew near, men passed their personal items, such as wallets, watches, letters, and pictures to those not making the charge and began final preparations. Another Federal chaplain remembered:

Our men here saw the danger, *yet were ready to face it.* Ere the hour set for the battle came, all my pockets and even haversack, were filled with sacred momentoes in case of death in the conflict — pocket-books, money, watches, lockets, rings, photographs. Each one as I passed by, or as he came and handed me his treasure or his keepsake, would say, in substance, "Chaplain, this is going to be a bloody business. In it the half of our regiment must no doubt fall, as we are in the front line. Of these, I may be one. . . . Take this, and should I fall, give or send it to such and such a loved one, telling them I fell with my face to the enemy, and this is to them — my last earthly momento and pledge of love!" During many of these, perhaps, final interviews, my emotions were unutterable, being only able to grasp the brave, generous hand, and turn away.[31]

As the signal cannons were fired and the artillery opened on the Federal right flank, the men grabbed their guns and silently fell into the ranks. They grimly awaited the bugle calls, signaling the attack. Anything, even charging into certain death, was better than this agonizing wait.[32]

General Warren spent the long, cold night preparing for the morning's attack. His front was about one mile long and his men deployed in one and two lines, amply supported. Brigadier General Henry D. Terry's division of the VI Corps anchored his left flank followed by the divisions of Brigadier General Alexander Hays, Brigadier General Alexander S. Webb, both of the II Corps, Prince and Carr, both of the III, and anchored on the right by Brigadier General John C. Caldwell of the II.

"I was thus prepared for strong and repeated assaults," Warren stated in his report, "with my flanks well guarded. Lieutenant-Colonel [Charles] Morgan, chief of staff, and myself, superintended this arrangement, and no part escaped our observation."[33]

With everything arranged, Warren took a few moments before dawn to sit around a campfire with a few staff officers. Reflecting on the events of the next morning, Warren told them, "If I succeed to-day I shall be the greatest man in the army; if I don't, all my sins will be remembered."[34]

At earliest dawn, Warren mounted and rode forward to study the Confederate line. It did not require his engineering expertise for him to realize immediately that the enemy had made significant fortification improvements during the night. He noted that at a run it would take his men at least eight minutes to reach the enemy line during which they "would be exposed to every species of fire."[35]

Warren was shaken by this discovery. Being too far from headquarters to seek Meade's advice before 8:00 a.m., Warren was faced with a great dilemma, the extent of which was noted by Captain Thomas Livermore of the II Corps:

> In command of nearly one half the army, the youngest major-general in it, with the hopes of General Meade resting upon his action, when to do nothing was almost as bad as a defeat; with such orders that the responsibility of defeat would have rested wholly or in great measure on General Meade; with a command full of courage, and believing that he would be the greatest man in the army, if he succeeded, he, as he afterwards said in my hearing, when he rode along his lines on that frigid morning and saw the enemy's position, thought of the wounded who were frozen at Fredericksburg and determined that he would not risk a defeat.[36]

Warren called off the attack.

As seemed to be the case with everyone else in his army, Meade had difficulty resting during the night. All orders had been issued and he was confident that Warren on his left and Sedgwick on his right had things well in hand. Yet so much depended on this attack. The success or failure of his campaign would be decided in the morning.

Meade and his staff rose early and rode to General Newton's headquarters to await the start of the attack. At approximately 8:00 a.m. they heard the signal gun fired followed by a number of 32-pound pieces along the line.[37] Through the brief pauses, the Federal commander intently listened for small arms fire on his left, but heard none.

Finally at about 8:50 a.m., after Meade had returned to his headquarters, a member of Warren's staff, Captain Washington Roebling,

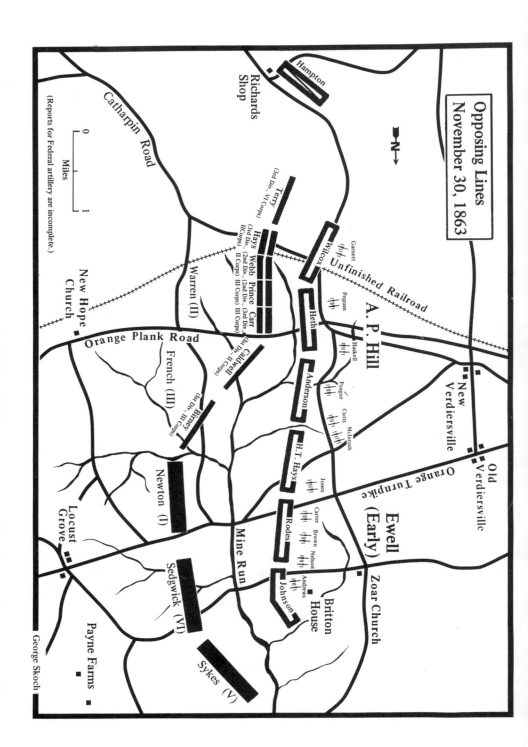

Opposing Lines
November 30, 1863

—N—→

George Skoch

78

galloped up to Meade's tent with the following message scribbled on a piece of paper: "[The enemy's] position and strength seem so formidable in my present front that I advise against making the attack here. The full light of the sun shows me that I cannot succeed."

Visibly unsettled by this news, Meade exclaimed, "My God! General Warren has half my army at his disposition!"[38] Captain Roebling further advised Meade that Warren had suspended the attack and would not mount one unless ordered.

"This was a terrible shock to all," Provost Marshal General Patrick recorded in his diary, "and Meade instantly ordered the whole movement to be suspended, sending off his Aids as fast as horses could carry them . . . ."[39]

Realizing that he did not have enough men on his right flank to adequately support an attack solely from that position, Meade sent couriers to Sedgwick to suspend his assault as well. With the attack only minutes away, staff officers galloped directly to VI Corps headquarters. They arrived just in time. The news came as a shock to Sedgwick and his staff since the enemy works on this flank were yet unfinished. They felt confident that an attack would succeed. Upon receiving Meade's order, however, Sedgwick informed his men to cease preparations for attack and suspended the artillery fire which was to have continued until the assault began.[40]

Meade, "looking as savage as anyone could,"[41] Humphreys and a few staff officers rode to the left to examine personally the enemy's position in Warren's front. After viewing the situation and determining that Warren's mind could not be changed, Meade decided not to overrule his corps commander and therefore officially cancelled the attack order.[42]

While riding back to headquarters, Meade was confronted by French, who was in a "fuming passion."[43] Upset by the fact that two of his divisions had been assigned to Warren for the attack which had now been scrapped, French tauntingly inquired of Meade, "Where are your young Napoleon's [Warren's] guns; why doesn't he open?"[44] After a brief exchange, and in no mood for a confrontation, the Federal commander continued to his headquarters.

That evening Meade held a council of war. Sedgwick reported that the artillery fire on the enemy left flank had exposed the Federal intention to attack at that point. The VI Corps commander had observed the Confederates strengthening that part of their line throughout the day, making it extremely formidable and leading him to report: "I do not believe the enemy's works can be carried in my front by an assault without numerous sacrifices. I regard the chances as three to one against the success of such an attack."[45]

The general weighed alternatives in an attempt to salvage some success from the campaign. The only option that initially seemed open to them was a renewed movement around the enemy's right flank. After further consideration, however, they realized that this would require support from the rest of the army and would also require abandoning the Orange Turnpike as the main line of communication. With provisions running low and the weather growing considerably colder and wet, Meade ruled out that alternative.[46]

One further option, the occupation of Fredericksburg, continued to be ruled out by Meade's superiors in Washington. "Had [Meade] done so," Humphreys later asserted, "the first battle with Lee, in May, 1864, would not have been fought in the Wilderness, but in a more open country."[47]

Exhausting all options, Meade reluctantly resolved to return north of the Rapidan on the evening of December 1. What had started out to be a very promising campaign strategy had failed miserably to achieve its primary objective — the defeat, or possibly the destruction, of the Army of Northern Virginia.

Confederate soldiers were well aware of the Federal intent to attack on the morning of November 30. They watched closely as a heavy line of Union skirmishers preceded strong enemy battle lines, while heavy Federal guns began to pound their works. As they studied the scene only a few hundred yards away, Lee's troops waited for the inevitable advance.

Secure behind their works, they in fact welcomed a Federal assault, knowing that their artillery covered the entire field. The Confederates looked forward to a slaughter reminiscent of Fredericksburg and a payback for their defeat in Pennsylvania. One member of the 12th Virginia Infantry recalled the events of that morning in a letter home.

> I never saw men so anxious for a fight as were ours — they *really rejoiced* when the Yankee line of battle emerged from the woods, threw out skirmishers, and started to advance, and it was with infinite regret that they saw them retire without assaying our position.[48]

When the Union attack failed to materialize by December 1, Lee decided to seize the initiative and assault the Federals the next morning. Since his army was considerably outnumbered, Lee surmised that Meade's reluctance to attack the day before meant that the Federal commander had either lost confidence in his plan — reminiscent of General Hooker's breakdown during the Battle of Chancellorsville which resulted in a Federal rout — or intended to abandon his line for a better tactical position closer to Richmond.[49]

Lee directed that Hill send Anderson's and Wilcox's divisions to the right, opposite the enemy left flank, which Stuart's scouts had discovered was relatively free of works. Early then extended his line south to fill in the gap created by the withdrawal of these two divisions.[50]

At dawn on December 2, Hill's men advanced, only to discover that the Army of the Potomac had abandoned the line and retreated north of the Rapidan. Just as Meade had dictated the start of the campaign, he also chose when to end it. A member of the 1st South Carolina Infantry recalled the mixed emotions of his fellow foot soldiers as they passed over the empty Yankee works:

> We all agreed that we would have carried their line, for they had scarcely any works, and our artillery would have very much commanded theirs. But still, we were too much worn out with rain and cold to have any great anxiety for further exertion . . . . it was voted no bad thing to be sent back to camp to rest.[51]

The Confederate commander did not share in his men's relief that the campaign was finally over. Although turning back the numerically superior enemy with fewer than 800 in losses, Lee had not achieved the decisive victory he had hoped would make up for the setbacks which seemed to be plaguing his command since the defeat at Gettysburg.

"I am too old to command this army," Lee angrily told his staff upon learning of the enemy retreat; "we should never have permitted these people to get away."[52] His anger led to depression over his failure to strike a decisive blow against Meade's army. It did not take long for him to come to terms with the manner in which the campaign ended. "I am greatly disappointed at his getting off with so little damage," he wrote to his wife two days later, "but we do not know what is best for us. I believe a kind God has ordered all things for our good. . . ."[53]

A great deal of dissatisfaction was also expressed in the Federal ranks. In a December 11, 1863, letter to a friend, Lieutenant Colonel Franklin Sawyer, commanding the 8th Ohio Infantry, evaluated the aftermath of the campaign.

> Meade has gone to Washington, I suppose to convince "Honest Old Abe" that he has perpetrated a good joke. (I think so) The Corps commanders are in a profound quarrel, as to their share of the glory or *in*glory, and all aspiring candidates for stars, here by superior strategy fell upon Washington, and laid siege to the Administration and Congress, which siege they are to press to an absolute surrender — You would be surprised to learn the great number of terrible attacks of "brigadier-on-the-brain" that here recently occurred in this army. It is indeed fearful.[54]

Specific blame for the failure was leveled in several different directions. French was censured for his delays on the 26th and 27th. The assertion that he was drunk throughout most of the campaign became an issue debated not only in the ranks but also in Northern newspapers. The consensus amongst the III Corps commander's peers and superiors was that, whether or not he was a drunk, French was certainly not corps commander material.[55]

French, on the other hand, pointed an accusing finger at General Prince. He alleged that the brigadier's habitual lateness caused the delays of the 26th and 27th.[56] It wouldn't be too long before both officers were relieved and assigned to different commands.

Surprisingly, Warren, who took it soley upon himself to suspend the battle which was to be the denouement of the campaign, escaped criticism from most quarters. In fact, many applauded the moral courage it took to decide to call off the attack. One veteran later reflected:

> That I live to write this is owing to the good judgment of General G. K. Warren; and I think, considering the nature of the man and circumstances under which he was placed, it required greater heroism to refuse the attack than to have led the charge in person.[57]

Lieutenant Colonel Jonathan H. Lockwood, commanding the 7th West Virginia Infantry, expressed the sentiments of the men of the II Corps in a December 5, 1863, letter to Warren: "When the orders came declining the hazardous task, it was felt and so expressed by officers and men as being one of the noblest acts of humanity on your part ever enacted. . . ."[58]

Although Warren suspended the attack, the final responsibility for the cancellation of the assault and the ultimate failure of the campaign rested squarely on Meade's shoulders. He was roundly criticized by the Northern press and felt that he would soon be relieved. He felt justified, however, that he had made the right decisions based on the circumstances throughout the campaign, particularly on the morning of November 30. In a letter written to his wife on the day his army recrossed the Rapidan, Meade stated:

> I therefore consider my fate as settled; but as I have told you before, I would rather be ignominiously dismissed, and suffer anything, than knowingly and wilfully have thousands of brave men slaughtered for nothing. It was my deliberate judgment that I ought not to attack; I acted on that judgment, and I am willing to stand or fall by it at all hazards.[59]

In his official report, Meade expressed the same thoughts he shared with his wife and proclaimed: ". . . I cannot be a party to a wanton slaughter of my troops for any mere personal end."[60]

Like his Confederate counterpart, Meade was greatly disappointed with the outcome of this campaign, especially since it had enjoyed such a promising beginning with the victories on the Rappahannock. Although the engagements of November 7 and the operation south of the Rapidan were both based on sound Federal plans, the reason for the latter's failure was that it was half-heartedly implemented by key subordinates. Also, Meade was not totally committed to his line of operations, which had been thrust on him by his superiors in Washington, preferring instead to launch his advance from the vicinity of Fredericksburg.

The Federal commander realized, however, that no matter who or what was to blame for the campaign's failure, he would be the person held accountable for its outcome. He was willing to assume the responsibility and awaited the decision of his superiors.

Having nothing to show for its losses — 172 men dead and more than 1450 wounded or missing — Meade's army retreated across the Rapidan to finally settle into its well-deserved winter encampment.

CHAPTER V

"Seems as Though They Are Never to be Conquered"

In the midst of a snow storm and growing darkness, a military train lumbered into Brandy Station at 4:00 p.m., Monday, February 15, 1864. Despite the cold blustery weather, the train's star passenger, Union Major General George Gordon Meade, was warmly greeted by his staff and other subordinates who had braved the chilly winter afternoon to meet Meade's train. About a month had passed since the commanding general had traveled to his home in Philadelphia, Pennsylvania, on a well-earned furlough. What Meade intended as a short visit had become a lengthy convalescence after he fell victim to pneumonia.[1]

While the general recuperated under the watchful eye of his family, the people of Philadelphia treated him to a hero's reception at Independence Hall. Meade took the opportunity to "pitch" for recruits. "The war," he said, "can be closed only by desperate and bloody fighting. What we want is fighting men to destroy the military power of the Rebels."[2]

Having recovered sufficiently to return to his troops, Meade left Philadelphia and arrived in Washington on February 12.[3] As always the capital was alive with rumors and political maneuverings, much of which dealt with Meade's future as commander of the Army of the Potomac.

At first it had seemed that Ulysses S. Grant might be a prime candidate to replace Meade, who was much maligned for a perceived lack of aggressive leadership, the latest example being the failure of the Mine Run Campaign. As it turned out, however, Lincoln had greater plans for Grant, his "Hero from the West." Within a month the President would promote the stoic cigar-wielding officer to the rank of lieutenant general, commanding all Federal armies.

Since the middle of January 1864, the rumor had been circulating around Washington and the army that Meade was about to be replaced by Brigadier General William F. "Baldy" Smith, a close friend of Grant. Smith had served in the Army of the Potomac before being transferred west. His stock as potential candidate to succeed Meade rose dramatically following the significant role he played in lifting the siege of Federal troops in Chattanooga, Tennessee, the previous fall.

Many general officers of the army still felt a strong allegiance to Meade. In addition, the idea that Lincoln would bring an officer already outranked by nine major generals in the Army of the Potomac, from the Western Theater to replace Meade caused great concern in the army and prompted General Marsena Patrick to remark: "This is producing much uneasiness in the minds of all who have the good of this Army at heart . . . ."[4]

Meade was reassured by Secretary of War Stanton on February 13 that he still had the confidence of the Lincoln administration. The general recounted his conversation with the secretary in a letter to his wife:

> The Secretary was, as he always is, very civil and ready to accede to all my suggestions. He gratified me very much by saying that there was no officer in command who had to so great a degree the implicit confidence of all parties as myself; but he said there were several officers in my army that did not have the confidence of the country, and that I was injuring myself by retaining them. I told him I did not know who they were, but that if he was aware of this fact, I thought it was his duty to retire them, and I should not object. . . .[5]

The next day Stanton and Meade further discussed the names of the officers who the secretary considered incompetent for their commands and how the army might be reorganized so that they could be replaced. The heavy losses of the I and III Corps at Gettysburg gave the secretary and general the opportunity to consolidate commands.

Discussions on this matter continued for more than a month and ultimately led to a general order on March 23 calling for the elimination of the I and III Corps, their components being redistributed between the II, V, and VI Corps. Generals French and Newton were relieved from command. With the return of Major General Winfield Scott Hancock, partially recovered from a serious wound received at Gettysburg, to take charge of his II Corps, Warren was permanently assigned the V Corps, replacing George Sykes.[6]

The performances of "Tardy" George Sykes and "Gin Barrel" William French during the Mine Run Campaign did nothing to enhance their reputations and save their positions. Henry Prince, although receiving a brief reprieve by his assignment to the 3rd Division, VI Corps, was relieved from command less than a month later.

Throughout the process of reorganization, Meade spoke up in behalf of his corps commanders, even French. Although he finally agreed to these moves, there was one proposed change to which he strongly objected — the dismissal of John Sedgwick from the command of the VI Corps.[7]

Meade first learned of Stanton's discontent with Sedgwick during their February 14 meeting. The primary cause was the VI Corps commander's handling of a joint military operation proposed by Major General Benjamin Butler in conjunction with the latter's XVIII Corps which was stationed at Fort Monroe on the tip of the Virginia Peninsula.

Butler, a criminal lawyer and Massachusetts state legislator with no prior military training, was, on May 16, 1861, the first major general of volunteers appointed by Lincoln. Although far from being a skilled military strategist, Butler's political connections helped him to wield considerable influence in the President's administration. During the winter of 1863-1864 he commanded the Federal Department of Virginia and North Carolina.[8]

In Meade's absence, Sedgwick, commanding the army, was less than enthusiastic in his support of Butler's plan, which had been backed by Halleck. When the operation failed, the administration felt that Sedgwick had not done his part to ensure its success.

Meade had great respect for the abilities of his VI Corps commander, so he must have been anxious to hear Sedgwick's side of this story. Meade prepared, therefore, to return to his army the next morning, February 15. He never needed much of an excuse to leave the capital. More accustomed to rustic regimental camp life after more than two and a half years of active campaigning, the Federal general tired easily of the fast paced, expensive Washington social life.

Upon his return to Brandy Station, Meade spent the evening catching up on the details of the past month, especially the aborted Butler-Sedgwick operation.

Piecing together what he had learned in Washington with the reports of his subordinates, Meade discovered that the operation was hatched by Butler upon being informed that Lee had sent 8,000 troops south to assist in a siege of Federal forces in New Berne, North Carolina.

On February 3, Butler wired Halleck requesting that the Army of the Potomac feint an advance across the Rapidan to force Lee to recall troops from North Carolina and/or the defenses around Richmond. Butler then proposed that he would advance up the Virginia Peninsula with 4,000 infantry, 2,200 cavalry, and two batteries of artillery in the hopes of capturing the Confederate capital long enough to free Federal troops imprisoned there. Butler received Halleck's blessing and was told to communicate directly with Sedgwick to coordinate the operation.[9]

On the evening of the 3rd, the acting commander of the Army of the Potomac received a ciphered dispatch from Butler requesting Sedgwick's cooperation. In his response, sent the next afternoon, Sedgwick informed Butler that he had greatly overestimated the number of troops which Lee had sent south. He also disagreed with Butler's assumption that a demonstration by the Army of the Potomac along the Rapidan would compel Lee to reduce the force guarding Richmond. "The condition of the roads and the present state of the weather," Sedgwick wired, "render an attempt at a flank movement impossible. The Rapidan in my front is so strongly intrenched that a demonstration upon it would not disturb Lee's army."[10]

Sedgwick's dispatch fell far short of being a strong endorsement of Butler's plan and led Butler to complain to Halleck that he "could get no co-operation from Sedgwick."[11]

On the morning of February 5, the general-in-chief ordered Sedgwick to give Butler as much cooperation as he could, to which the acting commander responded:

I will co-operate with General Butler as far as I can by vigorous demonstrations, and take advantage of such chances as may occur. A flank movement with this army is impossible in the present condition of the roads and state of the weather. Demonstrations in our front at the present time may, however, spoil the chances for the future.[12]

To his staff, Sedgwick was more succinct in his evaluation of Butler's plan. "Old Sedgwick and General Humpheys," Colonel Lyman stated in a letter to his wife, "are cross at the whole thing, looking on it as childish."[13]

Orders were hastily issued by Sedgwick for the next morning, February 6, calling for Brigadier General Wesley Merritt's cavalry division to demonstrate at Barnett's Ford on the Federal right flank and Brigadier General H. Judson Kilpatrick's at Culpeper Mine Ford on the left. The men of the I and II Corps were to be issued three days' rations and demonstrate along the northern bank of the Rapidan in the vicinity of Raccoon Ford and Morton's Ford respectively until the evening of the 8th, when they were to return to their camps. The III and VI Corps were to remain in reserve, ready to move at a moment's notice.[14]

Butler's force, under the command of Brigadier General Isaac J. Wistar, was to advance from Williamsburg on the road to Richmond early on the morning of the 6th.[15]

Operations on both fronts began on schedule. General Warren did not accompany his II Corps (General Hancock had not yet returned from his wound to assume its command) due to a minor illness which he was concerned could be aggravated by a cold rain which had been falling for several hours. Instead, the II Corps was led by General Caldwell, the 1st Division commander.

As Sedgwick had predicted, muddy roads slowed the march so that the three divisions of the II did not reach Morton's Ford until about 11:00 a.m.[16]

The ford was in the middle of a substantial bend, the convex side cutting into the northern bank. At this point the Rapidan was about 30 or 40 feet wide and about three to four feet deep. There was a small island between the two banks.[17]

Through a relatively thick fog, Caldwell and his staff could barely make out enemy rifle pits behind unfinished abatis across the river. From various points along the northern bank the Federals could see that the terrain behind the rifle pits gradually rose for about a mile where a high ridge, each end of which rested on the river, was fortified by Confederate troops and artillery.[18]

Warren's orders had been to demonstrate along the northern bank, feinting a crossing of the Rapidan. Either the II Corps commander failed to pass these directions on to his replacement or the latter chose to ignore them, for Caldwell directed Alexander Hays, commanding the 3rd Division, to send a small force across the river to capture the enemy rifle pits and secure the southern bank.[19]

Hays ordered Brigadier General Joshua T. Owen, commanding the division's 3rd Brigade, to choose 300 of his best troops for this assignment. The men quickly chosen, they charged through the mist into the cold water and raced across, dodging the fire of about 80 enemy pickets. Suffering no casualties, Owen's men captured 30 Confederates and secured the ford.

Owen personally led the rest of his brigade across the Rapidan, sending his troops to the right about three-quarters of a mile to a point just north of Dr. Morton's homestead. From this vantage point Owen could survey the strong enemy line and camps beyond. Not satisfied with this visual reconnaissance alone, however, he sent skirmishers forward to feel out the enemy position.

Shortly after his brigade reached Dr. Morton's house, Owen observed a heavy column of Confederate infantry deploying in his front. He communicated this information to his division commander, General Hays, who ordered his remaining two brigades across the Rapidan to support Owen's isolated command.[20]

One member of Colonel Samuel S. Carroll's Brigade recorded the men's reaction when ordered to cross the river:

> It was at this stage of the movement that our brave brigade commander, Colonel Carroll, rode along the brigade and intimated the part we were to play, by the laconic words, "Boys, you've got to take water." Caesar! how our under lip dropped and teeth chattered, and how the cold chills ran through us at the bare prospect of crossing that broad, deep river on a cold wintry day, and without the certainty of being able to dry our clothes when once across. But, notwithstanding, we 'grinned

and bore it,' though with many a shiver, and with more than one ejaculation smothered and outspoken.[21]

By 1:00 p.m. both the 1st and 2nd Brigades, commanded by Carroll and Colonel Charles Powers respectively, had crossed to Owen's support in the face of heavy enemy artillery fire. Owen shifted his brigade to the left, behind a ridge, and deployed Carroll's men behind his right flank and Powers behind his left.

General Hays crossed the Rapidan to assume command personally of his endangered force. Setting an example for his troops, the division commander dismounted and forded the cold river on foot. This 1844 West Point graduate was well liked by his men primarily for the example he set on the march and battlefield alike. He would unfortunately meet his fate less than three months later, during the early stage of Grant's Wilderness Campaign, while conspicuously directing troops along the Federal front.

Throughout the afternoon Hays watched as the enemy rushed reinforcements to the front from the vicinity of Clark's Mountain. Realizing the tenuous hold his division had on the southern bank, Hays kept Caldwell well informed of the enemy buildup.[22]

At about 3:00 p.m., Warren arrived at the ford to assume command of the corps. Quickly evaluating the situation, Warren decided that it would be a grave mistake to commit more troops across the Rapidan to join Hays' isolated command. In fact, he wished to withdraw Hays' division from the southern bank as soon as possible. There was a major problem, however. "He [the enemy] had complete control with his fire over the point of land our troops had gained on his side of the stream," Warren recounted in his report. "Our troops then were in a kind of cul-de-sac — a focus of fire." The II Corps commander realized that Hays would suffer heavy casualties from enemy artillery and small arms fire if he attempted to withdraw. The only hope for this segregated division was for Hays to somehow hold out until he could recross the river under cover of darkness — several hours away.[23]

Caldwell and Warren both had kept Sedgwick informed of developments at Morton's Ford. Surprised when he learned that elements of the II Corps had crossed the Rapidan, Sedgwick decided to take whatever advantage he could of this error, advising Caldwell to attack the enemy if he felt he cold do so without great loss.[24] Developments south of the ford, however, caused Warren to rule out any possibility of mounting an attack on the strong Confederate position.

Once apprised of Hays's situation south of the river, Sedgwick ordered Henry Prince's division of the III Corps to the ford as support for the II. The acting army commander then advised Newton, whose I Corps was by then deployed along the northern bank of the Rapidan at

Raccoon's Ford, almost three miles southwest of Morton's, to support Warren if necessary.

Both Merritt and Kilpatrick had crossed the river with portions of their commands to learn what they could about the enemy position. Sedgwick was less concerned about the safety of these mobile troopers than he was about the men of Hays' division.[25]

Once he learned of Warren's decision to withdraw Hays' force from their potential trap south of the ford, all Sedgwick could do was hope that darkness came before Lee had time to "gobble up" Hays' isolated command.

Following the end of the Mine Run Campaign, Lee's army had returned to its old defenses along the Rapidan. Ewell's Second Corps lay east of Clark's Mountain and Hill's Third to the west. With the army settling down into its winter camp, General Ewell, feeling sufficiently recovered from the lingering complications from the amputation of his leg, resumed command of his corps on December 4.[26]

Confederate President Jefferson Davis' administration reasoned that the retreat of the Federal army back across the Rapidan marked the end of the Army of Northern Virginia's active campaigning for the year. Lee was therefore called on to supply troops to assist in combating Union advances on three other fronts.

A Federal force under the command of Brigadier General William W. Averell began an advance from West Virginia into the Shenandoah Valley on December 8, 1863. General Butler's army of more than 25,000 men on the Virginia Peninsula posed a constant threat to the security of the Confederate capital. The third Union threat surfaced along the coast of North Carolina where Federals had built up a force of 11,000 soldiers.[27]

Having already sent James Longstreet's First Corps to the Western Theater, Lee hesitated to weaken his army any further with the enemy camped only a few miles away. Evaluating the situation on the other fronts, however, Lee realized that necessity dictated the need for the temporary transfer of some of his troops to reinforce the threatened Confederate forces.

The greatest threat existed in the Shenandoah Valley, the "breadbasket" of Lee's army. Not only were additional men necessary to reinforce the Confederate detachments there, but Lee realized that a strong general officer had to be sent under whose direction and leadership the various Confederate commands could be unified. Lee therefore chose Jubal A. Early for this crucial assignment.

The Confederate commander had been more than satisfied with Early's performance as a division leader and acting Second Corps commander. With this in mind, Lee directed Early in the middle of December to lead a detached force of infantry and cavalry from the Army of Northern Virginia to direct the defense of the Valley.[28]

Lee then turned his attention to the threat of Butler's troops against the defenses of Richmond. For that assignment Lee dispatched an infantry, cavalry, and artillery detachment of Maryland troops under the leadership of Colonel Bradley T. Johnson to the Confederate capital.[29]

To counter the threat posed by the Federals in North Carolina, Lee sent Brigadier General Robert F. Hoke's Tarheel Brigade, with the addition of the 43rd North Carolina and the 21st Georgia, to Major General George E. Pickett, commanding the Department of North Carolina.[30] The return to their native state was a welcome relief to Hoke's men. They had suffered through a trying and costly year which included their repulse on the slopes of Cemetery Hill on the second evening of the Battle of Gettysburg and their heavy losses at Rappahannock Station.

In addition to these transfers, furloughs, desertions, and losses during the Mine Run Campaign had reduced the number of men Lee had on hand at the end of January 1864 to fewer than 39,000, or about 10,000 fewer than he had had in the middle of the previous November. With a force of more than 86,000, the Army of the Potomac outnumbered Lee's force by better than two to one.[31]

Always vigilant to the movements of the enemy — one of the main reasons for his past successes — Lee wired the following message to President Davis on January 30, almost a week before Butler proposed his offensive operation to General Halleck:

> Report of a scout north of the Rappahannock gives movements of the enemy which generally precede an advance. . . . I do not think it can be a general advance of their army, but may be intended to distract or to co-operate with the movement reported in contemplation from Yorktown. . . . I have thought it proper to report these indications of some movement on the part of the enemy, as in the event of an advance upon the Peninsula I might not be able to detach troops toward Richmond, and other preparations should be made.[32]

Although Lee believed a Union advance might be at hand, he had no idea at what point along his extended, undermanned line the Federals would strike.

Early on the morning of February 6 it was quiet along the southern bank of the Rapidan. The First Company of Richmond Howitzers, under

First Lieutenant Robert Anderson, was posted to the right of the road heading southwest from the ford, about 800 yards from Dr. Morton's home.

At about 10:30 a.m., Anderson's men heard firing from the direction of the ford. Several minutes later, through the mist that shrouded the river valley, the artillerymen saw troops heading from the ford to Dr. Morton's. Thinking the shadowy figures were friendly pickets falling back, Anderson's men held their fire. Once Anderson was finally able to determine that the troops were indeed of the Federal variety, he ordered his men to open fire. As the alert gunners blasted away at the Yankees emerging from the ford, they also spied Federal batteries deploying on the high ground along the northern bank southwest of the ford and opened fire upon those enemy guns as well.

By chance, at the time the Federals were storming across the ford, George H. Steuart's Brigade was in the process of relieving two regiments each from the brigades of Brigadier General Stephen D. Ramseur and Brigadier General George Doles. As the Federals advanced from the ford, the troops from all three brigades rushed to the breastworks and prepared to repulse the enemy.[33]

General Ewell had established his headquarters less than three miles from the ford. When he received a dispatch from Anderson that the enemy had crossed the Rapidan, he rushed to the front. With the same fiery zeal he had exhibited on many battlefields early in the war — and which many associates thought had been extinguished with the loss of his leg — Ewell personally directed his infantry and artillery into position.[34]

Unsure of the strength of the enemy force crossing the river, Ewell called up all available troops from his corps to support his force manning the breastworks south of Morton's Ford. The Yankee prey had stumbled into a trap, and Ewell was anxious to spring it.

Hays' skirmishers kept up a constant fire throughout the afternoon with Ewell's troops in their front as Hays kept close watch over the activities along the enemy line.

As darkness neared, about 5:00 p.m., Ewell launched a three-pronged attack against the Federal line. While occupying the center of the Union position, Ewell hoped to turn either the enemy right or left flank, gain access to the roads leading to the ford, and encircle the enemy force.[35]

Hays' troops quickly reacted to the Confederate thrusts. On the right, Colonel Carroll bent his flank back to protect the Federal line and sent a heavy line of skirmishers forward to drive back the attacking enemy force.

One of Carroll's veterans later recalled:

"They are flanking us on the right; they are getting between us and the river," was now the startling cry. "Have you any orders for me?" cooly asked Colonel Carroll, of one of the aids. "No, Colonel, but they are flanking us on the right." "Then I'll take the responsibility to drive them back," replied the doughty Colonel, and then commanded, "Battalion! Right Face!! Forward—March!!" in those stentorian tones of his, which alone, seemingly, are enough to strike terror into a foe of usual stoicism.[36]

On the Federal left, Colonel Powers advanced the 14th Connecticut to regain the skirmish line. The 14th became intensely engaged and was reinforced by the 108th and 10th New York Infantry. The three regiments pushed the enemy force back more than 500 yards, past a group of buildings and trees, to the main Confederate line.[37]

Even darkness did not end the spirited contest. ". . .[T]he bright flashes from their guns," a Federal soldier recalled in a letter to a local newspaper, "presenting in the deepening gloom a splendid sight, though the contents of at least one-half of those iron tubes whistling, humming, and 'nipping' around was, to say the least, unpleasant."[38]

Perhaps remembering what the Confederates had encountered at Rappahannock Station only three months earlier, after darkness had fallen over the field, Warren feared for the security of Hays' men, especially in light of the aggressive enemy attack that afternoon. He therefore sent his 2nd Division, under General Webb, across the Rapidan to Hays' support until all Federal troops could safely be withdrawn to the northern bank.

Earlier in the day, a rough bridge had been built over the river. Webb's men quickly crossed this makeshift bridge and, masked from enemy guns by the darkness, rushed to the Federal line. Colonel DeWitt C. Baxter's 1st Brigade of Webb's division extended the Union right flank.

At 10:00 p.m., when Warren felt sure that his two divisions could safely fall back across the river, he ordered Hays to withdraw his troops. His pickets replaced by Baxter's brigade, Hays' men retreated to the northern bank. In his official report, Baxter stated:

It was now so dark that objects could not be distinguished at 10 paces. . . . Once the [picket] line was conducted to within less than 20 paces of the enemy's line, and, if it had not have drawn their fire, would in all probability have marched into and beyond their line without discovering the mistake in time to avert serious danger.[39]

Once Hays was across, Webb was directed to leave a small force to mask the retreat and return to the northern bank with the rest of his division.

About 2:30 a.m. the Confederates realized that the Federals were falling back across the Rapidan. Ewell's men advanced and drove the small group of Union skirmishers over the bridge to the main Federal line.

Unlike the disaster that befell the Confederate force at Rappahannock Station, Warren was able to extricate his command relatively untouched. Unlike that costly episode in November, the casualties suffered by both armies at Morton's Ford were relatively light. Warren's losses amounted to 11 killed, 204 wounded, and 40 captured or missing. Ewell lost 4 killed, 20 wounded, and more than 25 missing.[40]

Warren's men remained deployed along the heights of the northern bank throughout February 7, withdrawing that night to the camps they had left the day before. Although Sedgwick had initially intended to continue his demonstration along the Rapidan until the evening of the 8th, he determined that it was not having the intended effect on Lee's army and decided to return his infantry and cavalry to their camps on the 7th.[41]

Over 100 miles southeast of the Army of the Potomac, Butler's force, under the command of Brigadier General Isaac J. Wistar, left Williamsburg at 10:00 a.m. on February 6 for its raid on Richmond. Wistar's cavalry progressed rapidly toward the Confederate capital. At about 2:30 a.m. it reached Bottom's Bridge over the Chickahominy River, about 12 miles from the outskirts of Richmond.

A reconnaissance along the riverbank led the Federals to realize quickly that the enemy had expected them. "The bridge planks had been taken up," Wistar stated in his report, "the fords both above and below effectually obstructed, extensive earth-works and rifle-pits constructed, and a strong force of troops brought down by the York River Railroad, by which large accessions were still arriving."[42]

At daylight, the Federal cavalry attempted to charge across the Chickahominy but were easily repulsed. Realizing that the element of surprise had been lost, Wistar decided to abandon the raid and return to Williamsburg. Butler later claimed that a Union deserter who had been sentenced to death, but pardoned by Lincoln, had escaped and informed the enemy in advance of Wistar's raid.[43]

Butler's operation was bold but ill-conceived. Sedgwick did not attempt to mask his criticism of the plan, the weaknesses of which he felt were obvious and needed little explanation. He must have been taken aback, therefore, when he received the following dispatch from Halleck on February 11:

In your telegram of the 7th instant you say: "One result of the co-operation with General Butler has been to prove that it has

94

spoiled the best chance we had for a successful attack on the Rapidan."

The President directs that you report what this "best chance" was; what "successful attack" was proposed; when it was to be executed, and how it has been spoiled by your co-operation with General Butler.[44]

Sedgwick responded the next morning with a long, detailed explanation of his criticisms of Butler's plan. He claimed that he had not been given enough time to adequately prepare; the muddy roads prohibited rapid deployment of troops; and the demonstration revealed to Lee the inherent weakness in his defenses at Morton's Ford, causing him to strengthen that portion of his line.[45]

Lincoln and his War Department interpreted Sedgwick's remarks as being more critical of them than Butler and, consequently, considered relieving the VI Corps commander. Meade, however, had confidence in Sedgwick's ability and was able to retain him as a corps commander. This association was to be short lived. Little more than three months later Sedgwick was mortally wounded at Spotsylvania.

Meade hardly had a chance to settle back into the routine of command before he was informed by Stanton that the President had been conferring directly with one of Meade's subordinates, General Judson Kilpatrick, about another raid on Richmond.[46]

Lincoln had initially called Kilpatrick to Washington to discuss the distribution behind enemy lines of an amnesty proclamation for Confederate troops. This gave the cavalry commander an opportunity to propose to the President a raid on Richmond to free Federal prisoners.[47]

Lincoln was easily impressed by bold, aggressive plans, an element which he felt was sorely lacking in most of his military subordinates. He approved Kilpatrick's scheme and directed that everything be done to ensure its success.

Although lacking confidence in the plan, Meade had no choice but to obey the President's order. On February 28, the Federal general sent 1,500 troopers under Brigadier General George A. Custer west of Richmond and Sedgwick's VI Corps advanced toward Madison Court House. While these diversions occupied Lee's troops, Kilpatrick's 4,000 cavalrymen and a battery of light artillery crossed the Rapidan at Ely's Ford, slipped past the enemy line, and set a course for Richmond.[48]

Kilpatrick's troops reached the outskirts of Richmond on March 1 with little trouble, but found the enemy capital well defended along his front. Feeling that an attempt to force an entry into the city would meet with bloody failure, Kilpatrick reluctantly withdrew his force to General Butler's lines on the Peninsula, which he reached on March 3.[49]

In advance of his main column, Kilpatrick had sent a force of about 500 men under Colonel Ulric Dahlgren, the son of Federal Rear Admiral John A. Dahlgren, to seize the main bridge over the James River leading into the Confederate capital. On the night of March 1, Dahlgren and a small detachment of about 100 men became separated in the darkness from the rest of his command and were ambushed by Confederate cavalry. In the melee that followed Dahlgren was killed.[50]

Two controversial dispatches were discovered by Confederates in which Dahlgren directed his men to burn Richmond to the ground and assassinate Jefferson Davis and his cabinet.

The text of Dahlgren's papers was published across the South, inflaming citizens and soldiers alike to new levels of hatred toward the North. They also prompted Lee to send a rare communication to Meade requesting confirmation or denial of their authenticity. In his reply, Meade stated:

> . . . that neither the United States Government, myself, nor General Kilpatrick authorized, sanctioned, or approved the burning of the city of Richmond and the killing of Mr. Davis and cabinet, nor any other act not required by military necessity and in accordance with the usages of war.[51]

Meade called the whole affair "a pretty ugly piece of business. . . ."[52]

He did not have time to dwell on Butler's or Kilpatrick's failed missions, however, for an attack from a totally unexpected front threatened his position as commander of the Army of the Potomac to a far greater degree than any offensive yet launched by the enemy.

Meade related the substance of this "assault" in a letter to his wife on March 6.

> I returned from Washington to-day. I went there Friday [March 4] morning on business connected with the reorganization of the army . . . . When I reached Washington I was greatly surprised to find the whole town talking of certain grave charges of Generals Sickles and Doubleday, that had been made against me in their testimony before the Committee on the Conduct of the War. . . . Subsequently Mr. Stanton told me (this is strictly confidential), that there was and had been much pressure from a certain party to get Hooker back in command, and that thinking, through Sickles and others, they might get me out (a preliminary step) they had gotten up this halloobaloo in the Committee . . . ; but that I need not worry myself, there was no chance of their succeeding. The only evil that will result is the spreading over the country certain mysterious whisperings of dreadful deficiencies on my part, the truth concerning

which will never reach the thousandth part of those who hear the lies.[53]

Meade's letters home throughout March showed a preoccupation with the testimonies before the committee of such military luminaries as Abner Doubleday, Daniel Sickles and Daniel Butterfield,[54] each of whom held grudges against Meade: Doubleday for being superseded as commander of the I Corps by John Newton; Sickles for the criticisms lodged against him by Meade for his performance at the Battle of Gettysburg; and Butterfield for being replaced as Meade's chief of staff by Humphreys.

Although assured by Stanton that his position as commander of the Army of the Potomac was secure, Meade was very concerned about his reputation. He realized that no matter what anyone in the War Department said, his future was in the hands of Lieutenant General Ulysses S. Grant, who was officially named commander of all Federal armies on March 10.[55] Meade could be relieved by Grant at any time, so his reputation was all that he could rely on.

Meade appeared before the Committee on the Conduct of the War twice, on March 5 and again on the 12th, refuting many allegations introduced by his adversaries.[56] It wasn't Meade's testimony, however, which eventually reduced the ardor of the committee. Most of the members of the committee wished to have Meade replaced by Hooker, who was much closer to the political ideology of these politicians than was Meade. After Grant assumed command of the armies and chose to retain Meade, committee members realized it would be a waste of time to pursue the matter further, so they turned their attention to other matters.[57]

Grant decided to make his headquarters with the Army of the Potomac and to "advise" Meade on the best course of action to confront Lee's army. Once the lieutenant general arrived in the Eastern Theater, the attention and energies of Meade and his staff turned to working with Grant to plan the spring campaigns.

While all of the soldiers of the Army of the Potomac had a vested interest in the future of their commander, throughout the remainder of the winter of 1863-1864 they were far more concerned with making this brief respite from active campaigning as relaxing and enjoyable as possible.

Food and other supplies were plentiful and, once a soldier's corporal needs were met, he could give his full attention to other diversions. Popular pastimes included thespian and debating societies; regimental, brigade, and corps newspapers; card, chess, and checker games; cock fights; horse races; and religious services.

Dancing was another popular diversion in the army, especially for the officers. One of the most memorable events that winter was a ball staged by the officers of the II Corps on February 22, in celebration of George Washington's birthday. Attending were such luminaries as General Meade, Vice President Hannibal Hamlin, Secretary of the Interior John Usher, several senators, and all of the army's corps commanders with the exception of General French.[58] It was, wrote the usually dour Meade afterward, a "gay time."[59]

Although much fun was to be found in camp, furloughs home were preferred to anything else. Meade used the furlough process as an incentive to increase reenlistments by allowing any soldier who chose to remain in the army a thirty-day visit home. Whole units reenlisted and were granted furloughs together. The soldiers of the Army of the Potomac made the most of this winter respite. A few miles away, however, the attention of their opponents was focused more on survival than entertainment.

As always, shortages of food and clothing continued to plague the Army of Northern Virginia. The drastic decline in meat supplies — prompted by the loss of Trans-Mississippi cattle — for example, resulted in meager rations consisting largely of corn and potatoes. The average daily menu, usually limited to two meals, was monotonous. A breakfast of corn dodgers (boiled corn meal) and mashed potatoes was often followed by a supper of corn dodgers and watery soup. One soldier-chef described the "soup" as being ". . . made of water thickened with corn meal and mashed potatoes and cooked with a small piece of meat, which last, if salt, was taken out when the soup was done and kept to be cooked over again in the mashed potatoes for next morning's breakfast." Boiled rye, substituting for coffee, supplemented the meals.[60]

Staff officer McHenry Howard later recalled that during roll calls:

> . . . the sallow complexions and general appearance of the men indicated that they were insufficiently fed. . . . A soldier fighting for the best of causes should have, in his monotonous life, enough to eat as long as food will hold out issued in that way; he may put up with frequent irregularities, but if his ration be systematically insufficient for his appetite, his spirit and endurance must surely fail or become greatly impaired.[61]

Shortages were not limited to food items. They also included blankets, clothing, shoes, and forage for animals. Firewood was even scarce, requiring men to burn corn shucks for fuel.

Desertions increased not only because of supply deficiencies in the camps, but also because the men often received letters from loved ones "telling of dire distresses and apprehensions of worse in their families at home."[62] Furloughs were given whenever possible, but the thin ranks often necessitated denials of such requests, resulting in many desperate men going absent without leave.

General Lee, frustrated by the dismal conditions his beloved soldiers were forced to endure, relied on authorities in Richmond to ease the plight of his army. On January 22, 1864, he penned a dispatch to Confederate Secretary of War James Seddon:

A regular supply of provisions to the troops in this army is a matter of great importance. Short rations are having a bad effect upon the men, both morally and physically. Desertions to the enemy are becoming more frequent, and the men cannot continue healthy and vigorous if confined to this spare diet for any length of time. Unless there is a change, I fear the army cannot be kept effective, and probably cannot be kept together.[63]

Although their material needs suffered, Confederate soldiers were still encouraged to pursue religious activities to maintain their moral strength. Lee even went so far as to issue a general order on February 7 calling for "proper observance of the Sabbath" and its importance "not only as a moral and religious duty, but as contributing to the personal health and well-being of the troops."[64]

As rough as the winter was in the Confederate camps, life was not devoid of pleasure. Minstrel shows, sporting events, and games, particularly cards, were among their favorite forms of entertainment.

The idle soldiers also staged many snowball "battles" throughout the winter months. One of the more memorable seasonal contests occurred on March 23 when Early's division engaged Rodes' in the largest snowball fight of the winter. Even Generals Walker and Stafford participated. One of the veterans of the battle later recalled:

It was probably the greatest snowball battle ever fought, and showed that "men are but children of larger growth." The Richmond papers had several columns each giving an account of the battle. If all battles would terminate that way it would be a great improvement on the old slaughtering plan.[65]

The coming of spring instilled a new life into the troops of the Army of Northern Virginia. "The morning is bright and pleasant," one of Lee's soldiers recorded in his diary on the morning of May 4; "all nature seems smiling this spring morning. . . . The whole brigade is all life — seems as though they are never to be conquered."[66]

That evening, Lee's troops broke camp and headed east for their next meeting with the Army of the Potomac in the Wilderness. Things would be much different this time around, however, than when they last abandoned their camps to face Meade's troops along Mine Run only five months earlier. This spring the Federals were ably led by Lieutenant General Ulysses S. Grant, an aggressive leader who would not have to be coerced into action by his government. In fact, Grant would prove to be the most formidable foe the Lincoln administration would unleash against Lee and his Army of Northern Virginia.

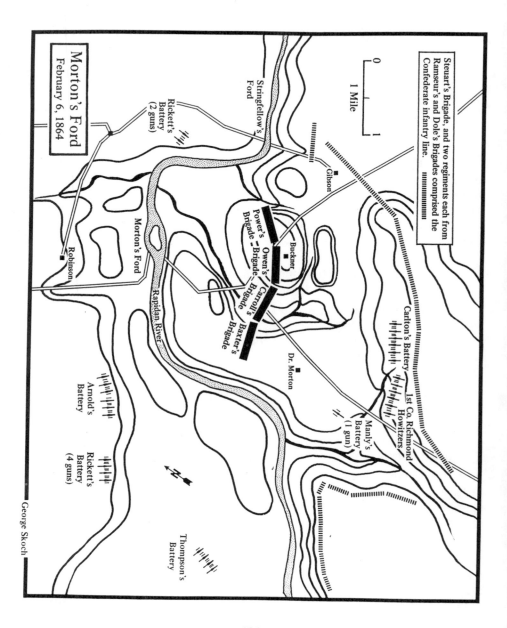

Morton's Ford
February 6, 1864

Steuart's Brigade, and two regiments each from Ramseur's and Dole's Brigades comprised the Confederate infantry line.

0   1 Mile

Stringfellow's Ford

Rickett's Battery (2 guns)

Gibson

Morton's Ford

Power's Brigade

Owen's Brigade

Carroll's Brigade

Baxter's Brigade

Buckner

Robinson

Rapidan River

Dr. Morton

Arnold's Battery

Rickett's Battery (4 guns)

Carlton's Battery

1st Co. Richmond Howitzers

Manly's Battery (1 gun)

Thompson's Battery

George Skoch

100

APPENDIX

Rappahannock Station
November 7, 1863
Casualty Lists

Units	Killed	Wounded	Missing	Total
FEDERAL				
V Corps-Sykes				
Bartlett's Div.	6	40	—	46
Ayres' Div.	1	5	5	11
Corps Total	7	45	5	57
VI Corps-Wright				
Russell's Div.	69	257	1	327
Howe's Div.	4	11	—	15
Terry's Div.	3	12	—	15
Corps Total	76	280	1	357
Artillery	—	5	—	5
FEDERAL TOTAL	83	330	6	419
CONFEDERATE				
Second Corps-Ewell				
Early's Div.				
Hays' Brig.	2	16	684	702
Hoke's Brig.	3	19	906	928
Green's Battery	1	—	41	42
CONFEDERATE TOTAL	6	35	1631	1672

Kelly's Ford
November 7, 1863
Casualty Lists

Units	Killed	Wounded	Missing	Total
FEDERAL				
III Corps-French				
Birney's Div.	5	34	—	39
Artillery	1	2	—	3
FEDERAL TOTAL	6	36	—	42

CONFEDERATE			
Second Corps-Ewell			
Rodes' Div.			
Daniel's Brig.	—	—	2	2
Dole's Brig.	—	5	—	5
Ramseur's Brig.	5	35	290	330
Battle's Brig.	—	2	15	17
Johnston's Brig.	—	3	2	5
CONFEDERATE TOTAL	5	45	309	359

Mine Run
November 26-December 2, 1863
Casualty Lists

Units	Killed	Wounded	Missing	Total
FEDERAL				
I Corps-Newton				
Cutler's Div.	3	33	7	43
Robinson's Div.	—	3	47	50
Corps Total	3	36	54	93
II Corps-Warren				
Caldwell's Div.	3	41	—	44
Webb's Div.	5	39	13	57
Hays' Div.	4	69	105	178
Monroe's Art. Brig.	—	3	—	3
Corps Total	12	152	118	282
III Corps-French				
Birney's Div.	29	287	17	333
Prince's Div.	27	136	37	200
Carr's Div.	69	320	10	399
Randolph's Art. Brig.	—	4	—	4
Corps Total	125	747	64	936
V Corps-Sykes				
Bartlett's Div.	—	7	19	26
Ayre's Div.	1	1	32	34
Crawford's Div.	2	7	2	11
Martin's Art. Brig.	1	4	8	13
Corps Total	4	19	61	84
VI Corps-Sedgwick				
Wright's Div.	—	9	—	9

Units	Killed	Wounded	Missing	Total
Terry's Div.	1	14	—	15
Tompkin's Art. Brig.	—	2	—	2
Corps Total	1	25	—	26
Cavalry Corps-Pleasonton				
Merritt's Div.	1	3	9	13
Gregg's Div.	25	108	57	190
Custer's Div.	—	3	4	7
Artillery	1	—	—	1
Corps Total	27	114	70	211
Artillery Corps-Hunt	—	1	—	1
FEDERAL TOTAL	172	1094	367	1633

Units	Killed	Wounded	Missing	Total
CONFEDERATES				
Second Corps-Early				
Early's Div.	8	43	28	79
Johnson's Div.	69	429	47	545
Rodes' Div.	8	25	12	45
Art. Battalion-Braxton	4	11	—	15
Corps Total	89	508	87	684
Third Corps-Hill				
Heth's Div.	8	37	30	75
Corps Total	8	37	30	75
Cavalry Corps-Stuart				
Hampton's Div.	9	22	—	31
Fitzhugh Lee's Div.	1	4	—	5
Corps Total	10	26	—	36
CONFEDERATE TOTAL	107	571	117	795

[Confederate Loss Reports are incomplete. Casualties for Walker's Brigade of Heth's Division were the only figures found for Hill's Corp.]

Morton's Ford
February 6, 1864
Casualty Lists

Units	Killed	Wounded	Missing	Total
FEDERAL				
II Corps-Caldwell/Warren				
Webb's Div.	—	2	—	2

Hays' Div.	11	201	40	252
Monroe's Art. Brig.	—	1	—	1
Corps Total	11	204	40	255
Cavalry Corps-Pleasonton				
Merritt's Div.	3	12	—	15
Corps Total	3	12	—	15
FEDERAL TOTAL	14	216	40	270
CONFEDERATE TOTAL	4	20	26	50

[Confederate totals were not broken down by units.]

ORGANIZATION OF THE ARMY OF NORTHERN VIRGINIA
NOVEMBER, 1863

SECOND ARMY CORPS
Lt. Gen. R. S. Ewell/
Maj. Gen. J. A. Early

EARLY'S DIVISION
Early/Brig. Gen. H. T. Hays

Pegram's Brigade
Brig. Gen. John Pegram
13th Virginia
31st Virginia
49th Virginia
52nd Virginia
58th Virginia

Gordon's Brigade
Brig. Gen. John Gordon
13th Georgia
26th Georgia
31st Georgia
38th Georgia
60th Georgia
61st Georgia

Hays' Brigade
Hays/Col. W. Monaghan
5th Louisiana
6th Louisiana
7th Louisiana
8th Louisiana
9th Louisiana

Hoke's Brigade
Hoke/Col. W. Monaghan
6th North Carolina
21st North Carolina
54th North Carolina
57th North Carolina
1st North Carolina Bn.
Sharpshooters

JOHNSON'S DIVISION
Maj. Gen. Edwd. Johnson

"Stonewall" Brigade
Brig. Gen. J. A. Walker

2nd Virginia
4th Virginia
5th Virginia
27th Virginia
33rd Virginia

Steuart's Brigade
Brig. Gen. George H. Steuart
1st Maryland Battalion
1st North Carolina
3rd North Carolina
10th Virginia
23rd Virginia
37th Virginia

Jones' Brigade
Brig. Gen. J. M. Jones
21st Virginia
25th Virginia
42nd Virginia
44th Virginia
48th Virginia
50th Virginia

Stafford's Brigade
Brig. Gen. L. A. Stafford
1st Louisiana
2nd Louisiana
10th Louisiana
14th Louisiana
15th Louisiana

RODES' DIVISION
Maj. Gen. R. E. Rodes

Daniel's Brigade
Brig. Gen. Junius Daniel
32nd North Carolina
43rd North Carolina
45th North Carolina
53rd North Carolina
2nd North Carolina Bn.

Ramseur's Brigade
Brig. Gen. S. D. Ramseur/
Col. W. R. Cox

2nd North Carolina
4th North Carolina
14th North Carolina
30th North Carolina

Dole's Brigade
Brig. Gen. George Doles
4th Georgia
12th Georgia
21st Georgia
44th Georgia

Battle's Brigade
Brig. Gen. C. A. Battle
3rd Alabama
5th Alabama
6th Alabama
12th Alabama
26th Alabama

Johnston's Brigade
Brig. Gen. R. D. Johnston
5th North Carolina
12th North Carolina
20th North Carolina
23rd North Carolina

THIRD ARMY CORPS
Lt. Gen. A. P. Hill

ANDERSON'S DIVISION
Maj. Gen. R. H. Anderson

Wilcox's Brigade
Col. J. C. C. Sanders
8th Alabama
9th Alabama
10th Alabama
11th Alabama
14th Alabama

Posey's Brigade
Brig. Gen. Carnot Posey
12th Mississippi
16th Mississippi

19th Mississippi
48th Mississippi

Mahone's Brigade
Brig. Gen. Wm. Mahone
6th Virginia
12th Virginia
16th Virginia
41st Virginia
61st Virginia

Wright's Brigade
Brig. Gen. A. R. Wright
3rd Georgia
22nd Georgia
48th Georgia
2nd Georgia Bn.

Perry's Brigade
Brig. Gen. E. A. Perry
2nd Florida
5th Florida
8th Florida

HETH'S DIVISION
Maj. Gen. Henry Heth

Davis' Brigade
Brig. Gen. J. R. Davis
2nd Mississippi
11th Mississippi
42nd Mississippi
55th North Carolina

Archer's Brigade
Brig. Gen. J. J. Archer
5th Alabama Bn.
13th Alabama
1st Tennessee (Prov.)
7th Tennessee
14th Tennessee

Walker's Brigade
Brig. Gen. H. H. Walker
40th Virginia
47th Virginia
55th Virginia
22nd Virginia Bn.

Kirkland's Brigade
Brig. Gen. W. W. Kirkland
11th North Carolina
26th North Carolina
44th North Carolina
47th North Carolina
52nd North Carolina

Cooke's Brigade
Brig. Gen. J. R. Cooke
15th North Carolina
27th North Carolina
46th North Carolina
48th North Carolina

WILCOX'S DIVISION
Maj. Gen. C. M. Wilcox

Lane's Brigade
Brig. Gen. J. H. Lane
7th North Carolina
18th North Carolina
28th North Carolina
33rd North Carolina
37th North Carolina

McGowan's Brigade
Brig. Gen. A. Perrin
1st South Carolina (Prov.)
12th South Carolina
13th South Carolina
14th South Carolina
Orr's (South Carolina) Rifles

Thomas' Brigade
Brig. Gen. E. L. Thomas
14th Georgia
35th Georgia
45th Georgia
49th Georgia

Scale's Brigade
Brig. Gen. A. M. Scales
13th North Carolina
16th North Carolina
22nd North Carolina
34th North Carolina
38th North Carolina

CAVALRY CORPS
Maj. Gen. J. E. B. Stuart

HAMPTON'S DIVISION
Maj. Gen. Wade Hampton

Gordon's Brigade
Brig. Gen. James B. Gordon
1st North Carolina
2nd North Carolina
4th North Carolina
5th North Carolina

Young's Brigade
Brig. Gen. P. M. B. Young
1st South Carolina
2nd South Carolina
Cobb's (Ga.) Legion
Jeff. Davis (Miss.) Legion
Phillips (Ga.) Legion

Rosser's Brigade
Brig. Gen. T. L. Rosser
7th Virginia
11th Virginia
12th Virginia
35th Virginia Bn.

FITZ. LEE'S DIVISION
Maj. Gen. Fitz. Lee

Lee's Brigade
Col. John R. Chambliss Jr.
9th Virginia
10th Virginia
13th Virginia

Lomax's Brigade
Brig. Gen. L. L. Lomax
1st Maryland Bn.
5th Virginia
6th Virginia
15th Virginia

Wickham's Brigade
Brig. Gen. W. C. Wickham
1st Virginia
2nd Virginia

3rd Virginia
4th Virginia

Artillery/Cavalry Corps
Maj. R. F. Beckham
Breathed's (Va.) Bat.
Hart's (S.C.) Bat.
Chew's (Va.) Bat.
McGregor's (Va.) Bat.
Moorman's (Va.) Bat.

ARTILLERY
Brig. Gen. W. N. Pendleton

SECOND ARMY CORPS
Brig. Gen. A. L. Long

Andrews' Battalion
Lt. Col. R. S. Andrews
1st Maryland Artillery
Chesapeake (Md.) Artillery
Alleghany (Va.) Artillery
Lee (Va.) Artillery

Carter's Battalion
Lt. Col. Thomas H. Carter
Jeff. Davis (Ala.) Artillery
King William (Va.) Artillery
Morris (Va.) Artillery
Orange (Va.) Artillery

Jones' Battalion
Lt. Col. Hilary P. Jones
Louisiana Guard Artillery

Charlottesville (Va.) Art.
Courtney (Va.) Artillery
Staunton (Va.) Artillery

Nelson's Battalion
Lt. Col. William Nelson
Milledge (Ga.) Artillery
Amherst (Va.) Artillery
Fluvanna (Va.) Artillery

1st Regiment Va. Art.
Col. J. Thompson Brown
2nd Rich. (Va.) Howitzers
3rd Rich. (Va.) Howitzers
Powhatan (Va.) Artillery
Rockbridge (Va.) Artillery
Salem (Va.) Flying Artillery

THIRD ARMY CORPS
Col. Reuben L. Walker

Cutt's Battalion
Lt. Col. Allen S. Cutts
Irwin (Ga.) Artillery
Patterson's (Ga.) Artillery
Ross' (Ga.) Artillery

McIntosh's Battalion
Maj. David G. McIntosh
Hardaway (Ala.) Battery
Danville (Va.) Artillery
Johnson's (Va.) Battery
2nd Rockbridge (Va.) Art.

Poague's Battalion
Maj. William T. Poague

Madison (Miss.) Artillery
Graham's (N.C.) Battery
Albemarle (Va.) Artillery
Brooke's (Va.) Battery

Garnett's Battalion
Lt. Col. John J. Garnett
Donaldsonville (La.) Art.
Huger (Va.) Artillery
Lewis (Va.) Artillery
Norfolk (Va.) Light Artillery

Pegram's Battalion
Maj. William J. Pegram
Pee Dee (S.C.) Artillery
Crenshaw (Va.) Battery
Fredericksburg (Va.) Art.
Letcher (Va.) Artillery
Purcell (Va.) Artillery

Haskell's Battalion
Maj. John C. Haskell
Branch (N.C.) Artillery
Rowan (N.C.) Artillery
Palmetto (S.C.) Artillery

RESERVE

Cabell's Battalion
Col. Henry C. Cabell
Callaway's (Ga.) Battery
Troup (Ga.) Artillery
Manly's (N.C.) Battery
1st Rich. (Va.) Howitzers
Nelson (Va.) Artillery

ORGANIZATION OF THE ARMY OF THE POTOMAC
NOVEMBER, 1863

FIRST ARMY CORPS
Maj. Gen. John Newton

FIRST DIVISION
Brig. Gen. S. Meredith

First Brigade
Brig. Gen. L. Cutler
19th Indiana

24th Michigan
1st New York Sharpshoot.
2nd Wisconsin
6th Wisconsin
7th Wisconsin

Second Brigade
Brig. Gen. J. C. Rice
7th Indiana

76th New York
84th New York (14th Mil.)
95th New York
147th New York
56th Pennsylvania

SECOND DIVISION
Brig. Gen. J. C. Robinson

First Brigade
Col. Samuel H. Leonard
16th Maine
13th Massachusetts
39th Massachusetts
94th New York
104th New York
107th Pennsylvania

Second Brigade
Brig. Gen. Henry Baxter
12th Massachusetts
83rd New York (9th Mil.)
97th New York
11th Pennsylvania
88th Pennsylvania
90th Pennsylvania

THIRD DIVISION
Brig. Gen. J. R. Kelly

First Brigade
Col. Chapman Biddle
121st Pennsylvania
142nd Pennsylvania

Second Brigade
Col. Langhorne Wister
143rd Pennsylvania
149th Pennsylvania
150th Pennsylvania

Third Brigade
Col. Nathan T. Dushane
1st Maryland
4th Maryland
7th Maryland
8th Maryland

ARTILLERY
Col. Charles S. Wainwright

Maine Light, 5th Bat. (E)
Maryland Light, Battery A
1st New York Light, Bat. H
1st N. Y. Light, Bats. E & L
1st Pennsyl. Light, Bat. B
4th United States, Bat. B

SECOND ARMY CORPS
Maj. Gen. G. K. Warren

FIRST DIVISION
Brig. Gen. J. C. Caldwell

First Brigade
Col. Nelson A. Miles
26th Michigan
61st New York
81st Pennsylvania
140th Pennsylvania

Second Brigade
Col. Patrick Kelly
28th Massachusetts
63rd New York
69th New York
88th New York
116th Pennsylvania (Bn.)

Third Brigade
Col. James A. Beaver
52nd New York
57th New York
66th New York
148th Pennsylvania

Fourth Brigade
Col. John R. Brooke
2nd Delaware
64th New York
53rd Pennsylvania
145th Pennsylvania

SECOND DIVISION
Brig. Gen. A. S. Webb

First Brigade
Col. DeWitt C. Baxter
19th Maine
15th Massachusetts
1st Minnesota
82nd N. Y. (2nd Militia)
152nd New York

Second Brigade
Col. Arthur F. Devereux

69th Pennsylvania
71st Pennsylvania
72nd Pennsylvania
106th Pennsylvania

Third Brigade
Col. Turner G. Morehead
19th Massachusetts
20th Massachusetts
7th Michigan
42nd New York
59th New York (Bn.)
1st Co. (Andrew) Mass.
Sharpshooters

THIRD DIVISION
Brig. Gen. A. Hays

First Brigade
Col. Samuel S. Carroll
14th Indiana
4th Ohio
8th Ohio
7th West Virginia (Bn.)

Second Brigade
Col. Thomas A. Smyth
14th Connecticut
1st Delaware
12th New Jersey
10th New York (Bn.)
108th New York

Third Brigade
Brig. Gen. Joshua T. Owen
39th New York
111th New York
125th New York
126th New York

ARTILLERY
Lt. Col. J. A. Monroe

1st New York Light, Bat. G
Pennsylvania Light, Bat. C
Pennsylvania Light, Bat. F
1st Pa. Light, Bats. F & G

1st R.I. Light, Bat. A.
1st R.I. Light, Bat. B.
5th United States, Bat. C

THIRD ARMY CORPS
Maj. Gen. W. H. French

FIRST DIVISION
Maj. Gen. D. B. Birney

First Brigade
Col. Charles H. T. Collis
57th Pennsylvania
63rd Pennsylvania
105th Pennsylvania
110th Pennsylvania
114th Pennsylvania
141st Pennsylvania

Second Brigade
Brig. Gen. J. H. H. Ward
3rd Maine
4th Maine
20th Indiana
86th New York
124th New York
99th Pennsylvania
2nd U.S. Sharpshooters

Third Brigade
Col. P. Regis de Trobriand
17th Maine
3rd Michigan
5th Michigan
40th New York
68th Pennsylvania
1st U.S. Sharpshooters

SECOND DIVISION
Brig. Gen. Henry Prince

First Brigade
Col. William Blaisdell
1st Massachusetts
11th Massachusetts
16th Massachusetts
11th New Jersey

26th Pennsylvania
84th Pennsylvania

Second Brigade
Col. William R. Brewster
70th New York
71st New York
72nd New York
73rd New York
74th New York
120th New York

Third Brigade
Brig. Gen. Gershom Mott
5th New Jersey
6th New Jersey
7th New Jersey
8th New Jersey
115th Pennsylvania

THIRD DIVISION
Brig. Gen. J. B. Carr

First Brigade
Brig. Gen. W. H. Morris
14th New Jersey
151st New York
10th Vermont

Second Brigade
Col. J. Warren Keifer
6th Maryland
110th Ohio
122nd Ohio
138th Pennsylvania

Third Brigade
Col. Benjmain F. Smith
106th New York
126th Ohio
67th Pennsylvania
87th Pennsylvania

ARTILLERY
Capt. G. E. Randolph

Maine Light, 4th Bat. (D)
Mass. Light, 10th Battery

N.H. Light, 1st Battery
N.J. Light, Battery B
1st N.Y. Light, Battery D
New York Light, 12th Bat.
1st R.I. Light, Battery E
4th United States, Bat. K

FIFTH ARMY CORPS
Maj. Gen. George Sykes

FIRST DIVISION
Brig. Gen. J. J. Bartlett

First Brigade
Col. William S. Tilton
18th Massachusetts
22nd Massachusetts
1st Michigan
118th Pennsylvania

Second Brigade
Col. Jacob B. Sweitzer
9th Massachusetts
32nd Massachusetts
4th Michigan
62nd Pennsylvania

Third Brigade
Col. Joseph Hays
20th Maine
16th Michigan
44th New York
83rd Pennsylvania

SECOND DIVISION
Brig. Gen. R. B. Ayres

First Brigade
Col. Sidney Burbank
3rd U.S. (six companies)
2nd U.S. (six companies)
11th United States
12th United States
14th United States
17th United States

Third Brigade
Brig. Gen. Kenner Garrard
140th New York
146th New York
91st Pennsylvania
155th Pennsylvania

THIRD DIVISION
Brig. Gen. S. W. Crawford

First Brigade
Col. William McCandless
1st Pennsylvania Reserves
2nd Pennsylvania Reserves
6th Pennsylvania Reserves
13th Pennsylvania Reserves

Third Brigade
Col. Martin D. Hardin
5th Pennsylvania Reserves
9th Pennsylvania Reserves
10th Pennsylvania Reserves
11th Pennsylvania Reserves
12th Pennsylvania Reserves

ARTILLERY
Capt. Augustus P. Martin

Mass. Light, 3rd Battery (C)
Mass. Light, 5th Battery (E)
1st N.Y. Light, Battery C
1st Ohio Light, Battery L
3rd U.S., Batteries F & K
5th U.S., Battery D

SIXTH ARMY CORPS
Maj. Gen. John Sedgwick

FIRST DIVISION
Brig. Gen. H. G. Wright/
Brig. Gen. David Russell
First Brigade
Brig. Gen. A. T. A. Torbert
1st New Jersey
2nd New Jersey
3rd New Jersey
4th New Jersey
15th New Jersey

Second Brigade
Col. Emory Upton
5th Maine
121st New York
95th Pennsylvania
96th Pennsylvania

Third Brigade
Col. Peter C. Ellmaker
6th Maine
49th Pennsylvania
119th Pennsylvania
5th Wisconsin

SECOND DIVISION
Brig. Gen. A. P. Howe

Second Brigade
Col. Lewis A. Grant
2nd Vermont
3rd Vermont
4th Vermont
5th Vermont
6th Vermont

Third Brigade
Brig. Gen. Thomas H. Neill
7th Maine
43rd New York
49th New York
77th New York
61st Pennsylvania

THIRD DIVISION
Brig. Gen. H. D. Terry

First Brigade
Brig. Gen. Alexan. Shaler
65th New York
67th New York
122nd New York
23rd Pennsylvania
82nd Pennsylvania

Second Brigade
Brig. Gen. Henry L. Eustis
7th Massachusetts
10th Massachusetts

37th Massachusetts
2nd Rhode Island

Third Brigade
Brig. Gen. Frank Wheaton
62nd New York
93rd Pennsylvania
98th Pennsylvania
102nd Pennsylvania
139th Pennsylvania

ARTILLERY
Col. Charles H. Tompkins

Mass. Light, 1st Bat. (A)
New York Light, 1st Bat.
1st R.I. Light, Battery C
1st R.I. Light, Battery G
New York Light, 3rd Bat.
4th United States, Bat. C
5th United States, Bat. F
5th United States, Bat. M

CAVALRY CORPS
Maj. Gen. A. Pleasonton

FIRST DIVISION
Brig. Gen. John Buford

First Brigade
Col. George H. Chapman
8th Illinois
3rd Indiana
8th New York

Second Brigade
Col. Thomas C. Devin
4th New York
6th New York
9th New York
17th Pennsylvania
3rd West Virginia

Reserve Brigade
Brig. Gen. W. Merritt
19th New York
6th Pennsylvania

1st United States
2nd United States
5th United States

SECOND BRIGADE
Brig. Gen. D. McM. Gregg

First Brigade
Col. John P. Taylor
1st Massachusetts
1st New Jersey
6th Ohio
1st Pennsylvania
3rd Pennsylvania
1st Rhode Island

Second Brigade
Col. J. Irvin Gregg
1st Maine
10th New York
2nd Pennsylvania
4th Pennsylvania
8th Pennsylvania
13th Pennsylvania
16th Pennsylvania

THIRD DIVISION
Brig. Gen. G. A. Custer

First Brigade
Brig. Gen. H. E. Davies, Jr.
2nd New York
5th New York
18th Pennsylvania
1st West Virginia

Second Brigade
Col. Charles H. Town

1st Michigan
5th Michigan
6th Michigan
7th Michigan
1st Vermont

UNATTACHED/GUARDS

4th Pennsylvania (detach.)
16th Pennsylvania (detach.)
10th New York, Company M
13th Pennsylvania, Co. G
1st Vermont (detachment)
6th United States
1st Ohio, Companies A & C

ARTILLERY
Brig. Gen. H. J. Hunt

ARTILLERY RESERVE
Brig. Gen. R. O. Tyler

First Volunteer Brigade
Lt. Col. Freeman McGilvery
Maine Light, 6th Battery
Mass. Light, 9th Battery
New York Light, 4th Bat.
1st Ohio Light, Battery H

Second Volunteer Brigade
Capt. Elijah D. Taft
1st Conn. Heavy, Bat. B
1st Conn. Heavy, Bat. M
1st N.Y. Light, Battery B
New York Light, 5th Bat.
West Va. Light, Battery C

Third Volunteer Brigade
Maj. Robert H. Fitzhugh
New Jersey Light, Bat. A
1st N.Y. Light, Battery K
New York Light, 15th Bat.
1st United States, Bat. H

First Brigade Horse Art.
Capt. James Robertson
New York Light, 6th Bat.
2nd U.S., Batteries B & L
2nd United States, Bat. D
2nd United States, Bat. M
4th United States, Bat. A
4th United States, Bat E

Second Brigade Horse Art.
1st United States, Bat. E
1st United States, Bat. I
1st United States, Bat. K
2nd United States, Bat.A
2nd United States, Bat. G
3rd United States, Bat. C

Ammunition Guard
6th New York Heavy Art.

PROVOST GUARD
Brig. Gen. M. R. Patrick

1st Maryland Cavalry
80th New York (20th Mil.)
93rd New York
1st U.S. Cavalry (Squad.)

111

BIBLIOGRAPHY
Books

Agassiz, George R., ed. *Meade's Headquarters, 1863-1865: Letters of Colonel Theodore Lyman from the Wilderness to Appomattox.* Boston: The Atlantic Monthly Press, 1922.

Ambrose, Stephen E. *Upton and the Army.* Baton Rouge: Louisiana State University Press, 1964.

Baquet, Camille. *History of the First Brigade, New Jersey Volunteers, from 1861 to 1865.* Trenton: Mac Crellish and Quigley Printer, 1910.

Best, Isaac O. *History of the 121st New York State Infantry.* Chicago: Lieutenant James Smith, 1921.

Blake, Henry N. *Three Years in the Army of the Potomac.* Boston: Lee and Shepard, 1865.

Buck, Samuel D. *With the Old Confeds: Actual Experience of a Captain in the Line.* Baltimore: H. E. Houck & Co., 1925.

Caldwell, J. F. J. *The History of a Brigade of South Carolinians Known as "Gregg's," and Subsequently as "McGowan's Brigade."* Philadelphia: King & Baird, 1866.

Carter, Robert G., ed. *Four Brothers in Blue.* Austin: University of Texas Press, 1978.

Casler, John O. *Four Years in the Stonewall Brigade.* Marietta, Ga.: Continental Book Co., 1951.

Chapla, John D. *42nd Virginia Infantry.* Lynchburg, Va.: H. E. Howard, Inc., 1983.

Clark, Walter, Ed. *Histories of the Several Regiments and Battalions from North Carolina in the Great War, 1861-'65.* 5 vols. Raleigh, N.C.: E. M. Uzzell, 1901.

Cleaves, Freeman. *Meade of Gettysburg.* Norman: University of Oklahoma Press, 1960.

Early, Jubal A. *Autobiographical Sketch and Narrative of the War Between the States.* Philadelphia: J. B. Lippincott Co., 1912.

Fisk, Wilbur. *Anti-Rebel: The Civil War Letters of Wilbur Fisk.* Croton-on-Hudson, New York: Emil Rosenblatt, 1983.

Fox, William F. *Regimental Losses in the American Civil War, 1861-1865.* Albany, New York: Albany Publishing Co., 1889.

Freeman, Douglas S. *Lee's Lieutenants: A Study in Command.* 3 vols. New York: Charles Scribner's Sons, 1943-1944.

_____*R. E. Lee: A Biography.* 4 vols. New York: Charles Scribner's Sons, 1934-1935.

History of the 118th Pennsylvania Volunteers, Corn Exchange Regiment: From Their First Engagement at Antietam to Appomattox. Philadelphia: J. L. Smith, 1905.

Howard, McHenry. *Recollections of a Maryland Confederate Soldier and Staff Officer.* Baltimore: Williams & Wilkins, Co., 1914.

Humphreys, Andrew A. *From Gettysburg to the Rapidan: The Army of the Potomac: July, 1863, to April, 1864.* New York: Charles Scribner's Sons, 1883.

The James Sprunt Historical Studies. 60 vols. Chapel Hill: The University of North Carolina Press, 1900-1987.

Johnson, Robert U., and Buel, Clarence C., eds. *Battles and Leaders of the Civil War.* 4 vols. New York: The Century Co., 1884, 1888.

Jones, J. Williams, et. al., ed. *Southern Historical Society Papers.* 52 vols. and 2 vol. index. 1876-1959.

Jones, Terry L. *Lee's Tigers: The Louisiana Infantry in the Army of Northern Virginia.* Baton Rouge: Louisiana State University Press, 1987.

Kepler, William. *History of the Three Months' and Three Years' Service, from April 16, 1861, to June 22d, 1864, of the Fourth Regiment Ohio Volunteer Infantry in the War for the Union.* Cleveland: Leader Printing Co., 1886.

Lee, Laura Elizabeth. *Forget-Me-Nots of the Civil War.* St. Louis, Mo.: Press A. R. Fleming Printing Co., 1909.

Lee, Robert E. *Recollections and Letters of General Robert E. Lee.* Garden City, New York: Doubleday, Page & Co., 1924.

Lewis, George. *The History of Battery E, First Regiment, Rhode Island Light Artillery.* Providence: Snow & Farnham, 1892.

Livermore, Thomas L. *Days and Events, 1860-1866.* Boston: Houghton Mifflin Co., 1920.

McCarthy, Carlton. *Detailed Minutiae of Soldier Life in the Army of Northern Virginia.* Richmond: C. McCarthy and Co., 1882.

Mark, Penrose. *Red: White: and Blue Badge, Pennsylvania Veteran Volunteers. A History of the 93d Regiment, Known as the "Lebanon Infantry. . .".* Harrisburg: Aughinbaugh Press, 1911.

Meade, George G., ed. *The Life and Letters of George Gordon Meade.* 2 vols. New York: Charles Scribner's Sons, 1913.

Meier, Heinz K., ed. *Memoirs of a Swiss Officer in the American Civil War.* Bern, Switzerland: Herbert Lang and Co., 1972.

Michie, Peter S. *The Life and Letters of Emory Upton.* New York: D. Appleton and Co., 1885.

Military Historical Society of Massachusetts. *Papers.* 14 vols. Boston: Houghton Mifflin Co., 1895-1918.

Military Order of the Loyal Legion of the United States: Iowa Commandery. *War Sketches and Incidents as Related by Companions of the . . . .* 2 vols. Des Moines: P. C. Kenyon Press, 1893, 1898.

Moore, Edward A. *The Story of a Cannoneer Under Stonewall Jackson.* New York: The Neale Publishing Co., 1907.

Nevins, Allan, ed., *A Diary of Battle: The Personal Journals of Colonel Charles S. Wainwright, 1861-1865.* New York: Harcourt, Brace & World, 1962.

Paris, Louis Philippe Albert D'Orleans, Comte de. *History of the Civil War in America.* 4 vols. Philadelphia: J. H. Coates and Co., 1875-1888.

Pennypacker, Isaac R. *Great Commanders: General Meade.* New York: D. Appleton and Co., 1901.

Ray, Frederick E. *Alfred R. Waud: Civil War Artist.* New York: Viking Press, 1974.

Robertson, James I. *4th Virginia Infantry.* Lynchburg, Va.: H. E. Howard, Inc., 1982.

Sloan, John A. *Reminiscence of the Guilford Grays, Co. B, 27th N. C. Regiment.* Washington: R. O. Polkinhorn, 1883.

Sparks, David S. *Inside Lincoln's Army: The Diary of Marsena Rudolph Patrick, Provost Marshal General, Army of the Potomac.* New York: Thomas Yoseloff, 1964.

Stafford, Dr. G. M. G. *General Leroy Augustus Stafford: His Forebears and Descendants.* New Orleans: Pelican Publishing Co., 1943.

Stevens, Charles A. *Berdan's United States Sharpshooters in the Army of the Potomac, 1861-1865.* St. Paul, Minn.: Price McGill Co., 1892.

Stewart, Rev. A. M. *Camp, March, and Battlefield.* Philadelphia: James B. Rodgers, 1865.

Taylor, Walter H. *Four Years with General Lee.* New York: D. Appleton and Co., 1877.

Trobriand, Regis de. *Four Years with the Army of the Potomac.* Boston: Ticknor & Co., 1889.

Tyler, Mason W. *Recollections of the Civil War.* New York: G. P. Putnam's Sons, 1912.

U.S. Congress. *Report of the Joint Committee on the Conduct of the War.* 8 vols. Milwood, New York: Kraus Reprint Co., 1977.

U.S. War Department, comp. *War of the Rebellion: A Compilation of the Official Records of the Union and Confederate Armies.* 128 vols. Washington: Government Printing Office, 1880-1901.

Walker, Francis A. *History of the Second Army Corps of the Army of the Potomac.* New York: Charles Scribner's Sons, 1891.

Warner, Ezra J. *Generals in Blue.* Baton Rouge: Louisiana State University Press, 1964.

———*Generals in Gray.* Baton Route: Louisiana State University Press, 1959.

Welles, Gideon. *Diary of Gideon Welles.* 3 vols. Boston: Houghton Mifflin Co., 1911.

Whitman, William E. S., and True, Charles H. *Maine in the War for the Union: A History of the Part Borne by Maine Troops in the Suppression of the American Rebellion.* Lewiston: Nelson Dingley Jr. & Co., 1865.

Williams, T. Harry. *Lincoln and His Generals.* New York: Alfred A. Knopf, Inc., 1952.

Winslow, Richard Elliott, III. *General John Sedgwick: The Story of a Union Corps Commander.* Novato, Calif.: Presidio Press, 1982.

Wise, George. *Campaigns and Battles of the Army of Northern Virginia.* New York: The Neale Publishing Co., 1916.

Worsham, John H. *One of Jackson's Foot Cavalry: His Experience and What He Saw During the War, 1861-1865.* New York: The Neale Publishing Co., 1912.

Periodicals

Luvaas, Jay and Nye, Wilbur. "The Campaign That History Forgot." *Civil War Times Illustrated.* November, 1969.

Skoch, George. "The Man Who Fed the South." *Civil War Times Illustrated.* November, 1983.

Wert, Jeffery. "Rappahannock Station." *Civil War Times Illustrated.* December, 1976.

Newspapers

National Tribune (Washington, D.C.), 1883, 1887, 1890.
New York Times, 1864.
New York World, 1863.
Richmond Daily Dispatch, 1863.
Vincennes (Ind.) *Western Sun,* 1863.

Maps

U.S. Department of the Interior. Geological Survey. National Mapping Division.

Manuscripts

Batchelor, Albert A., Papers. Louisiana and Lower Mississippi Valley Collections. LSU Libraries. Louisiana State University.

Edwards, Leroy S., Papers. Archives Collection. Randolph Macon College.

Fisk, Wilbur, Collection. Manuscript Division. Library of Congress.

Grimes, J. Bryan, Papers. Southern Historical Collection. Wilson Library, University of North Carolina at Chapel Hill.

Heth, Henry, Papers. Eleanor S. Brockenbrough Library. The Museum of the Confederacy. Richmond, Va.

Lyman, Theodore, Papers and Diary. Massachusetts Historical Society. Boston.

McElvany, James Thomas, Letters and Journal. Possession of John and Robert Bailey. Austell, Georgia.

Patrick, Marsena R., Papers. Manuscript Division. Library of Congress.

Saunders, Fleming, Papers. Manuscript Division. Virginia Historical Society.

Sexton, Samuel, Papers. Manuscript Division. Ohio Historical Society. Columbus.

Seymour, William J., Journal. Schoff Civil War Collection. William L. Clements Library. University of Michigan.

Warren, Gouverneur K., Papers. New York State Library. Albany.

ENDNOTES

Chapter I

1. *The War of the Rebellion: A Compilation of the Official Records of the Union and Confederate Armies* (Washington, D.C.: 1880-1901) Series 1, Vol. XXIX, pt. 1, 250, 428. (Cited hereafter as *O.R.* Unless otherwise noted, all volumes are from Series 1.)
2. John A. Sloan, *Reminiscences of the Guilford Grays* (Washington, D.C.: 1883), 74.
3. George R. Agassiz, ed., *Meade's Headquarters 1863-1865* (Boston: 1922), 36-37.
4. Ezra J. Warner, *Generals in Blue* (Baton Rouge: 1964), 196.
5. *O.R.,* Vol. XXIX, pt. 2, 346.
6. Agassiz, *Meade's Headquarters,* 36.
7. *Diary of Gideon Welles* (Boston: 1911), Vol. I, 438-440.
8. *O.R.,* Vol. XXIX, pt. 2, 346.
9. *Ibid.,* 354.
10. *Ibid.,* 361-362.
11. Agassiz, *Meade's Headquarters,* 37.
12. George Meade, ed., *The Life and Letters of George Gordon Meade* (New York: 1913), Vol. II, 154. (All citings will be from Vol. II).
13. T. Harry Williams, *Lincoln and His Generals* (New York: 1952), 288.
14. Meade, *Life and Letters,* 154.
15. *O.R.,* Vol. XXIX, pt. 2, 375.
16. Robert E. Lee, *Recollections and Letters of General Robert E. Lee* (Garden City, N.Y.: 1924), 113-114.
17. *Richmond Daily Dispatch,* November 5, 1863.
18. *O.R.,* Vol. XXIX, pt. 1, 587-589; U.S. Geological Survey Map — Remington, Virginia Quadrangle.
19. *O.R.,* Vol. XXIX, pt. 1, 619-620.
20. *Ibid.,* 611, 618.
21. *Ibid.,* 619-620.
22. Meade, *Life and Letters,* 154.
23. Freeman Cleaves, *Meade of Gettysburg* (Norman, Oklahoma: 1960), 202.
24. *O.R.,* Vol. XXIX, pt. 2, 409.
25. *Ibid.,* 412.
26. *Ibid.,* 425-426.
27. Agassiz, *Meade's Headquarters,* 36.
28. *O.R.,* Vol. XXIX, pt. 1, 631-633.
29. Ezra J. Warner, *Generals in Gray* (Baton Rouge: 1959), 64.
30. *O.R.,* Vol. XXIX, pt. 1, 566, 568-574.
31. Frederick E. Ray, *Alfred R. Waud: Civil War Artist* (New York: 1974), 143.
32. *O.R.,* Vol. XXIX, pt. 1, 633.
33. George Lewis, *The History of Battery E, First Rhode Island Light Artillery* (Providence, R.I.: 1892), 239.
34. Heinz K. Meier, ed., *Memoirs of a Swiss Officer in the American Civil War* (Bern, Switzerland: 1972), 129.
35. Charles A. Stevens, *Berdan's United States Sharpshooters* (St. Paul, Minn.: 1892), 369.

36. Regis de Trobriand, *Four Years with the Army of the Potomac* (Boston: 1889), 549.
37. *O.R.,* Vol. XXIX, pt. 1, 561, 632.
38. Warner, *Generals in Blue,* 417.
39. *O.R.,* Vol. XXIX, pt. 1, 578, 587-589.
40. *History of the 118th Pennsylvania Volunteers, Corn Exchange Regiment* (Philadelphia: 1881), 338.
41. Richard Elliott Winslow III, *General John Sedgwick: The Story of a Union Corps Commander* (Novato, Calif.: 1982), 122.
42. Edward A. Moore, *The Story of a Cannoneer Under Stonewall Jackson* (New York: 1907), 206.
43. George Wise, *Campaigns and Battles of the Army of Northern Virginia* (New York: 1916), 290.
44. *O.R.,* Vol. XXIX, pt. 1, 589, 627.
45. William J. Seymour Journal, Diary Entry: November 7, 1863, University of Michigan.
46. *O.R.,* Vol. XXIX, pt. 1, 226, 628.
47. *History of the Corn Exchange Regiment,* 339.
48. *O.R.,* Vol. XXIX, pt. 1, 577, 583, 599, 607.
49. *Ibid.,* 621, 629-630.
50. Walter Clark, ed., *Histories of the Several Regiments and Battalions from North Carolina in the Great War 1861-"65* (Raleigh: 1901), Vol. III, 273.
51. Warner, *Generals in Gray,* 108.
52. *O.R.,* Vol. XXIX, pt. 1, 585.
53. *O.R.,* Vol. XXIX, pt. 2, 430-434.
54. *O.R.,* Vol. XXIX, pt. 1, 585.
55. Robert U. Johnson and Clarence C. Buel, ed., *Battles and Leaders of the Civil War* (New York: 1884, 1888), Vol. IV, 86.
56. *O.R.,* Vol. XXIX, pt. 1, 588.
57. *Ibid.,* 585.
58. *Ibid.,* 589.
59. William F. Fox, *Regimental Losses in the American Civil War 1861-1865* (Albany, N.Y.: 1889), 128, 395.
60. *O.R.,* Vol. XXIX, pt. 1, 588.
61. William Whitman and Charles True, *Maine in the War for the Union* (Lewiston, Me.: 1865), 158.
62. Seymour Journal, Diary Entry: November 7, 1863.
63. Charles A. Clark, "Campaigning with the 6th Maine," *War Sketches and Incidents as Related by Companions of the Iowa Commandery, Military Order of the Loyal Legion of the United States* (Des Moines, Iowa: 1898), Vol. II, 47.
64. *Ibid.,* 49. Jeffery Wert, "Rappahannock Station," *Civil War Times Illustrated* (hereafter cited *CWTI*), December, 1976, 45.
65. *History of the Corn Exchange Regiment,* 343.
66. Clark, *History of the Several Regiments and Battalions from North Carolina,* Vol. I, 319.
67. *O.R.,* Vol. XXIX, pt. 1, 589, 597-599, 623, 628, 630.
68. Penrose Mark, *Red: White: and Blue Badge, Pennsylvania Veteran Volunteers. A History of the 93d Regiment, Known as the "Lebanon Infantry. . . "* (Harrisburg: 1911), 232.

69. Albert A. Batchelor Papers, December 21, 1863. Letter from Charles Batchelor to his father, Louisiana State University.
70. Camille Baquet, *History of the First Brigade, New Jersey Volunteers, from 1861 to 1865* (Trenton: 1910), 102.
71. *O.R.*, Vol. XXIX, pt. 1, 589, 592, 594, 600-601.
72. Stephen E. Ambrose, *Upton and the Army* (Baton Rouge: 1964), 25; Peter S. Michie, *The Life and Letters of Emory Upton* (New York: 1885), 83-85; Isaac O. Best, *History of the 121st New York State Infantry* (Chicago: 1921), 102.
73. *O.R.*, Vol. XXIX, pt. 1, 623-624.
74. Terry Jones, *Lee's Tigers* (Baton Rouge: 1987), 184.
75. *Ibid.*, 184.
76. *Ibid.*, 184.
77. *O.R.*, Vol. XXIX, pt. 1, 625.
78. *Ibid.*, 613, 621-622.
79. *Ibid.*, 622.
80. Samuel D. Buck, *With the Old Confeds: Actual Experiences of a Captain in the Line* (Baltimore: 1925), 94-98.
81. Comte de Paris, *History of the Civil War in America* (Philadelphia: 1883), Vol. III, 795.
82. *O.R.*, Vol. XXIX, pt. 1, 625, 629-630, 632.
83. *Ibid.*, 559, 561, 575.
84. Walter H. Taylor, *Four Years with General Lee* (New York: 1877), 116.
85. Douglas S. Freeman, *Lee's Lieutenants* (New York: 1944), Vol. III, 267.
86. *O.R.*, Vol. XXIX, pt. 1, 625.
87. Seymour Journal, Diary Entry: November 7, 1863.
88. *O.R.*, Vol. XXIX, pt. 1, 612-613.
89. Winslow, *General John Sedgwick*, 124.
90. Meade, *Life and Letters*, 155.
91. *O.R.*, Vol. XXIX, pt. 2, 443.
92. Johnson and Buel, *Battles and Leaders*, Vol. IV, 87.
93. Jones, *Lee's Tigers*, 187.

Chapter II

1. Douglas S. Freeman, *R. E. Lee: A Biography* (New York: 1935), Vol. III, 191-192.
2. Clark, *Histories of the Several Regiments and Battalions from North Carolina*, Vol. IV, 186.
3. Carlton McCarthy, *Detailed Minutiae of Soldier Life in the Army of Northern Virginia* (Richmond: 1882), 26.
4. Robert E. Park, "War Diary of Captain Robert Emory Park," *Southern Historical Society Papers* Vol. XXVI, 23. (Cited hereafter as *SHSP*.)
5. *O.R.*, Vol. XXIX, pt. 2, 434-435.
6. *O.R.*, Vol. XXIX, pt. 1, 563-564.
7. *O.R.*, Vol. XXIX, pt. 2, 435.
8. De Trobriand, *Four Years with the Army of the Potomac*, 550.
9. David S. Sparks, ed., *Inside Lincoln's Army*, (New York: 1964), 304.
10. Agassiz, *Meade's Headquarters*, 45.
11. *O.R.*, Vol. XXIX, pt. 1, 553.

12. Sparks, *Inside Lincoln's Army,* 305.
13. Meade, *Life and Letters,* 170-176.
14. U.S. Congress, *Report of the Joint Committee on the Conduct of the War* (Milwood, N.Y.: 1977), Vol. IV, 372.
15. *Ibid.,* 385.
16. John H. Worsham, *One of Jackson's Foot Cavalry* (New York: 1912), 184.
17. Leroy S. Edwards Papers, November 10, 1863. Letter from Leroy Edwards to his father, Randolph Macon College.
18. De Paris, *Civil War in America,* Vol. III, 797-798.
19. George Skoch, "The Man Who Fed the South," *CWTI,* November, 1983, 44.
20. *O.R.,* Vol. XXIX, pt. 2, 830, 832-833.
21. John D. Chapla, *42nd Virginia Infantry* (Lynchburg: 1983), 39-40.
22. Lee, *Recollections and Letters,* 116.
23. *O.R.,* Vol. XXIX, pt. 2, 832.
24. Sparks, *Inside Lincoln's Army,* 313; *Richmond Daily Dispatch,* November 27, 1863; J. Bryan Grimes Papers, November 23, 1863, letter from Bryan Grimes to his wife, University of North Carolina at Chapel Hill.
25. Allan Nevins, ed., *A Diary of Battle: The Personal Journals of Colonel Charles S. Wainwright 1861-1865* (New York: 1962), 301.
26. Agassiz, *Meade's Headquarters,* 47.
27. *New York World,* November 12, 1863; Johnson and Buel, *Battles and Leaders,* Vol. IV, 87-88n.
28. *O.R.,* Vol. XXIX, pt. 2, 449.
29. Winslow, *General John Sedgwick,* 125.
30. *O.R.,* Vol. XXIX, pt. 2, 454.
31. *Ibid.,* 459-461.
32. Winslow, *General John Sedgwick,* 125.
33. Sparks, *Inside Lincoln's Army,* 308.
34. *Ibid.,* 307.
35. *O.R.,* Vol. XXIX, pt. 2, 473-474.
36. *Ibid.,* 474.
37. *O.R.,* Vol. XXIX, pt. 1, 13, 677.
38. *Ibid.,* 13.
39. *Ibid.,* 13-14; *O.R.,* Vol. XXIX, pt. 2, 480-481.
40. Cleaves, *Meade of Gettysburg,* 207.
41. Andrew A. Humphreys, *From Gettysburg to the Rapidan: The Army of the Potomac: July, 1863 to April, 1864* (New York: 1883), 50.
42. Wilbur Fisk, *Anti-Rebel: The Civil War Letters of Wilbur Fisk* (Croton-on-Hudson, N.Y.; 1983), 167.
43. Humphreys, *From Gettysburg to the Rapidan,* 50; *O.R.,* Vol. XXIX, pt. 2, 481-482.
44. Fisk, *Anti-Rebel,* 167.
45. *O.R.,* Vol. XXIX, pt. 2, 846.

Chapter III

1. *O.R.,* Vol. XXIX, pt. 1, 736, 737, 760-761.
2. *Ibid.,* 737-739.
3. *Ibid.,* 768.
4. *Ibid.,* 761.

5. *Ibid.,* 14, 694, 794.
6. *O.R.,* Vol. XXIX, pt. 2, 491.
7. *O.R.,* Vol. XXIX, pt. 1, 694-695, 738.
8. Agassiz, *Meade's Headquarters,* 53.
9. *O.R.,* Vol. XXIX, pt. 2, 489.
10. Humphreys, *From Gettysburg to the Rapidan,* 50.
11. *Ibid.,* 53.
12. *O.R.,* Vol. XXIX, pt. 1, 830.
13. *Ibid.,* 827.
14. *Ibid.,* 827.
15. J. F. J. Caldwell, *The History of a Brigade of South Carolinians* (Philadelphia: 1866), 118; November 27, 1863 Entry, "The Letters and Journals of Major James Thomas McElvany of the Georgia 35th Infantry Regiment," unpublished typescript. Freeman, *R. E. Lee: A Biography,* Vol. III, 195.
16. *O.R.,* Vol. XXIX, pt. 1, 730-731, 838-839.
17. *Ibid.,* 839.
18. *Ibid.,* 877.
19. *Ibid.,* 695.
20. *Ibid.,* 794, 806-807, 898-899.
21. Henry H. Walker's Official Report of the Action, Unpublished, Henry Heth Papers, Museum of the Confederacy.
22. Warner, *Generals in Blue,* 493.
23. *O.R.,* Vol. XXIX, pt. 1, 895-897.
24. *Ibid.,* 29.
25. Humphreys, *From Gettysburg to the Rapidan,* 57.
26. *Ibid.,* 58-59; *O.R.,* Vol. XXIX, pt. 1, 762.
27. *Ibid.,* 738-739.
28. Henry Blake, *Three Years in the Army of the Potomac* (Boston: 1865), 256-257; George B. Davis, "The Bristoe and Mine Run Campaigns," *Papers of the Military Historical Society of Massachusetts,* Volume III, *Campaigns in Virginia, Maryland and Pennsylvania: 1862-1863* (Boston: 1903), 497-99. (Cited hereafter as *MHSM.*)
29. Jay Luvaas and Wilbur S. Nye, "The Campaign that History Forgot," *CWTI,* November, 1969, 36.
30. *O.R.,* Vol. XXIX, pt. 2, 498.
31. *O.R.,* Vol. XXIX, pt. 1, 762.
32. *O.R.,* Vol. XXIX, pt. 2, 498, 500.
33. *Ibid.,* 500.
34. *O.R.,* Vol. XXIX, pt. 1, 762.
35. *Ibid.,* 762-763.
36. *O.R.,* Vol. XXIX, pt. 2, 501.
37. Sparks, *Inside Lincoln's Army,* 314.
38. *O.R.,* Vol. XXIX, pt. 1, 846.
39. Warner, *Generals in Gray,* 158.
40. *O.R.,* Vol. XXIX, pt. 1, 846-849.
41. Clark, *Histories of the Several Regiments and Battalions from North Carolina,* Vol. I, 198.
42. *O.R.,* Vol. XXIX, pt. 1, 763.

43. *Ibid.,* 763.
44. *Ibid.,* 742.
45. Isaac R. Pennypacker, *Great Commanders: General Meade* (New York: 1901), 250.
46. *O.R.,* Vol. XXIX, pt. 1, 856, 863.
47. Worsham, *One of Jackson's Foot Cavalry,* 188.
48. *O.R.,* Vol. XXIX, pt. 1, 848.
49. Dr. G. M. G. Stafford, *General Leroy Augustus Stafford* (New Orleans: 1943), 42-43.
50. McHenry Howard, *Recollections of a Maryland Confederate Soldier and Staff Officer* (Baltimore: 1914), 242.
51. *Ibid.,* 242.
52. *O.R.,* Vol. XXIX, pt. 1, 742-743, 746, 847.
53. Jubal A. Early, *Autobiographical Sketch and Narrative of the War Between the States* (Philadelphia: 1912), 321.
54. *O.R.,* Vol. XXIX, pt. 1, 15-16.
55. *Ibid.,* 828-829.
56. Park, "War Diary of Captain Robert Emory Park," *SHSP,* Volume XXVI, 24.

Chapter IV

1. Agassiz, *Meade's Headquarters,* 55.
2. *O.R.,* Vol. XXIX, pt. 1, 16.
3. Vincennes (Ind.) *Western Sun,* December 19, 1863.
4. *O.R.,* Vol. XXIX, pt. 1, 696.
5. Sparks, *Inside Lincoln's Army,* 317.
6. Davis, "The Bristoe and Mine Run Campaign," *MHSM,* Vol. III, 500.
7. *O.R.,* Vol. XXIX, pt. 1, 829, 834, 848, 896.
8. *Ibid.,* 807, 829, 899-900.
9. *Ibid.,* 696.
10. *Ibid.,* 697.
11. Francis A. Walker, *History of the Second Army Corps* (New York: 1886), 379.
12. *O.R.,* Vol. XXIX, pt. 1, 697.
13. *Report of the Joint Committee on the Conduct of the War,* Vol. IV, 386.
14. *O.R.,* Vol. XXIX, pt. 1, 16.
15. Meade, *Life and Letters,* 157.
16. *O.R.,* Vol. XXIX, pt. 1, 16-17.
17. De Paris, *Civil War in America,* Vol. III, 809.
18. H. M. Wagstaff, "The James A. Graham Papers, 1861-1884," *The James Sprunt Historical Studies,* Vol. XX, #2, (Chapel Hill, N.C.: 1928), 171.
19. William Kepler, *History of the Three Months' and Three Years' Service, from April 16, 1861, to June 22d, 1864, of the Fourth Regiment Ohio Volunteer Infantry in the War for the Union* (Cleveland: 1886), 150.
20. Fleming Saunders Papers, November 30, 1863, letter from Fleming Saunders to his mother, Virginia Historical Society.
21. Laura Elizabeth Lee, *Forget-Me-Nots of the Civil War* (St. Louis, 1909), 101.
22. Luvaas, "The Campaign that History Forgot," *CWTI,* 32.
23. Robert G. Carter, ed., *Four Brothers in Blue* (Austin, Texas: 1978), 373.
24. *History of the Corn Exchange Regiment,* 371.

25. Mason W. Tyler, *Recollections of the Civil War* (New York: 1912), 127.
26. Robert E. Bigbee, "More About Mine Run," *National Tribune,* July 26, 1883.
27. Vincennes (Ind.) *Western Sun,* December 19, 1863.
28. H. S. Stevens, "Those Slips of Paper: Another Graphic Account," *National Tribune,* July 12, 1883.
29. M. R. Johnson, "Those Slips of Paper: Another Graphic Account," *National Tribune,* July 12, 1883.
30. Thomas L. Livermore, *Days and Events, 1860-1866* (Boston: 1920), 302; Bigbee, *National Tribune,* July 26, 1883.
31. Rev. A. M. Stewart, *Camp, March and Battlefield* (Philadelphia: 1865), 365.
32. Kepler, *Fourth Regiment Ohio Volunteer Infantry,* 150.
33. *O.R.,* Vol. XXIX, pt. 1, 698.
34. Livermore, *Days and Events,* 301.
35. *O.R.,* Vol. XXIX, pt. 1, 698.
36. Livermore, *Days and Events,* 304.
37. Agassiz, *Meade's Headquarters,* 56.
38. *O.R.,* Vol. XXIX, pt. 2, 517; Agassiz, *Meade's Headquarters,* 56.
39. Sparks, *Inside Lincoln's Army,* 317.
40. Winslow, *General John Sedgwick,* 131.
41. Livermore, *Days and Events,* 303.
42. Walker, *History of the Second Army Corps,* 385.
43. Agassiz, *Meade's Headquarters,* 57.
44. Livermore, *Days and Events,* 304.
45. *O.R.,* Vol. XXIX, pt. 2, 929.
46. *O.R.,* Vol. XXIX, pt. 1, 17.
47. Humphreys, *From Gettysburg to the Rapidan,* 68.
48. Edwards Papers, November 29, 1863, letter from Leroy Edwards to his father.
49. De Paris, *Civil War in America,* Vol. III, 812.
50. *O.R.,* Vol. XXIX, pt. 1, 896, 900.
51. Caldwell, *The History of a Brigade of South Carolinians,* 120.
52. Johnson and Buel, *Battles and Leaders,* Volume IV, 240.
53. Lee, *Recollections and Letters,* 116.
54. Samuel Sexton Papers, December 11, 1863, letter from Franklin Sawyer to Samuel Sexton, Ohio Historical Society.
55. Gouverneur Warren Papers, December 3, 1863. Letter from Warren to Andrew Humphreys and letters to the *New York Tribune* from officers of the III Corps and Major General John Sedgwick, New York State Library.
56. *O.R.,* Vol. XXIX, pt. 1, 739.
57. Bigbee, *National Tribune,* July 26, 1883.
58. Warren Papers.
59. Meade, *Life and Letters,* 158.
60. *O.R.,* Vol. XXIX, pt. 1, 18.

Chapter V

1. Meade, *Life and Letters,* 165.
2. Cleaves, *Meade of Gettysburg,* 219-220.
3. *Ibid.,* 220.
4. Sparks, *Inside Lincoln's Army,* 330.

5. Meade, *Life and Letters,* 165.
6. *O.R.,* Vol. XXXIII, 717-718.
7. Meade, *Life and Letters, 185.*
8. Warner, *Generals in Blue,* 60-61.
9. *O.R.,* Vol. XXXIII, 506-507; Humphreys, *From Gettysburg to the Rapidan,* 73.
10. *O.R.,* Vol. XXXIII, 502, 512-513.
11. *Ibid.,* 519.
12. *Ibid.,* 514.
13. Agassiz, *Meade's Headquarters,* 68.
14. *O.R.,* Vol. XXXIII, 515-516.
15. *Ibid.,* 145.
16. *Ibid.,* 119-120, 123.
17. W. D. Taylor, "Morton's Ford, Va.," *National Tribune,* September 18, 1890.
18. *O.R.,* Vol. XXXIII, 115, 127.
19. Humphreys, *From Gettysburg to the Rapidan,* 73.
20. *O.R.,* Vol. XXXIII, 127, 133.
21. Kepler, *Fourth Regiment Ohio Volunteer Infantry,* 155.
22. *O.R.,* Vol. XXXIII, 127.
23. *Ibid.,* 115.
24. *Ibid.,* 524.
25. *Ibid.,* 139-141.
26. *O.R.,* Vol. XXIX, pt. 2, 859.
27. *O.R.,* Vol. XXIX, pt. 1, 919 and Vol. XXXIII, 482.
28. *O.R.,* Vol. XXIX, pt. 1, 970-971 and pt. 2, 876, 901.
29. *O.R.,* Vol. XXIX, pt. 2, 905.
30. *O.R.,* Vol. XXXIII, 1099, 1202.
31. *Ibid.,* 462, 1135.
32. *Ibid.,* 1131.
33. *Ibid.,* 141-143.
34. Freeman, *Lee's Lieutenants,* Vol. III, 334.
35. *O.R.,* Vol. XXXIII, 128-129, 133.
36. Kepler, *Fourth Regiment Ohio Volunteer Infantry,* 156.
37. *O.R.,* Vol. XXXIII, 129.
38. Vincennes (Ind.) *Western Sun,* February 20, 1864.
39. *O.R.,* Vol. XXXIII, 122.
40. *Ibid.,* 118, 141.
41. *Ibid.,* 532.
42. *Ibid.,* 146-147.
43. *Ibid.,* 144.
44. *Ibid.,* 552.
45. *Ibid.,* 553-554.
46. *Ibid.,* 170.
47. *Ibid.,* 172.
48. *Ibid.,* 170.
49. *Ibid.,* 181-187.
50. *Ibid.,* 194-197.
51. *Ibid.,* 178-180.
52. Meade, *Life and Letters,* 190-191.

53. *Ibid.,* 169-170.
54. *Ibid.,* 170-185.
55. *O.R.,* Vol. XXXIII, 663.
56. *Ibid.,* 169, 177.
57. *Ibid.,* 175.
58. *National Tribune,* April 21, 1887; *New York Times,* February 26, 1864.
59. Meade, *Life and Letters,* 167.
60. Howard, *Recollections of a Maryland Confederate Soldier and Staff Officer,* 253.
61. *Ibid.,* 252.
62. *Ibid.,* 254.
63. *O.R.,* Vol. XXXIII, 1114.
64. *Ibid.,* 1150.
65. John O. Casler, *Four Years in the Stonewall Brigade* (Marietta, Ga.: 1951), 204.
66. James I. Robertson, *4th Virginia Infantry* (Lynchburg: 1982), 31.

INDEX

127

Mine Run:
A Campaign Of Lost Opportunities

October 21, 1863 -May 1, 1864

Martin F. Graham   George F. Skoch